EBB TIDE

By SPENCER BIDWELL KING, JR.

Illustrations by WILLIAM ETSEL SNOWDEN, JR.

EBB TIDE

*As Seen Through the Diary of
Josephine Clay Habersham
1863*

UNIVERSITY OF GEORGIA PRESS
Athens   1958

Paperback edition, 2009
© 1958 by the University of Georgia Press
Athens, Georgia 30602
www.ugapress.org
All rights reserved
Printed digitally in the United States of America

The Library of Congress has cataloged the hardcover edition of this book as follows:
Library of Congress Cataloging-in-Publication Data

Habersham, Josephine Clay Habersham, 1821–1893.
Ebb tide; as seen through the diary of Josephine Clay Habersham, 1863. By Spencer Bidwell King,
Jr. Illus. by William Etsel Snowden, Jr.
129 p. illus. 22 cm.
1. Habersham family. 2. United States—History—Civil War, 1861–1865— Personal narratives,
Confederate.
3. Savannah (Ga.)—Social life and customs. I. King, Spencer Bidwell.
E605 .H115
973.782   58-59847

Paperback ISBN-13: 978-0-8203-3447-9
ISBN-10: 0-8203-3447-2

To the Memory of

JOSEPHINE NOBLE JONES CRISFIELD
1872-1953

MARY SAVAGE JONES ANDERSON
1873-1958

CONTENTS

Preface	ix
Avon	1
The Foreshadowing	21
Turning of the Tide	33
Fire in the Ashes	57
Tears in Their Eyes	77
Solace at Christ Church	91
Ah, My Poor Princes	107
Index	124

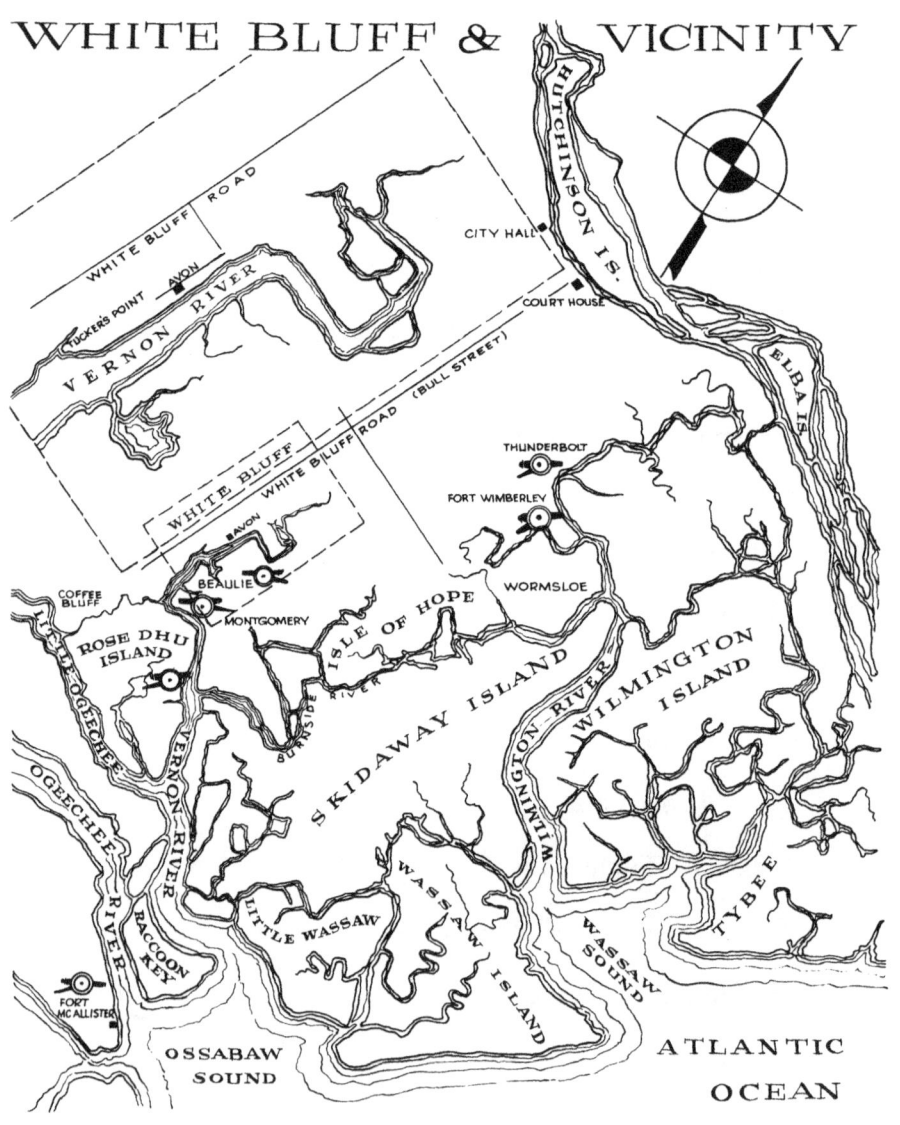

PREFACE

THE HEART of *Ebb Tide* is the diary of Josephine Clay Habersham which she kept in 1863. The story is particularly one of life and death in wartime as it affected the Habersham family; but it has broader implications than can be found in Savannah, the home of this eminent Georgia family. It reaches up the South Carolina coast to Hilton Head, Port Royal, Beaufort, and as far as Fort Sumter in Charleston Harbor, surrounded by batteries and forts on James, Morris, and Sullivan's islands; and it reaches down the coast of Georgia from Fort Pulaski at the mouth of the Savannah River to Fort McAllister on the Ogeechee. It stretches north to Gettysburg and west to Jackson and Vicksburg. It follows Sherman from Chattanooga to Atlanta and, finally, to Savannah—that exquisite relic of colonial culture that was too fine for the soiled hands of the sons of war to defile. It is the story of a Southern aristocrat of noble lineage who was humbled and disciplined by defeat. Through this woman's triumph of faith we see Southern womanhood spiritually victorious in the face of physical defeat. We see the ebbing of the tide on the Vernon River as a symbol of the ebbing tide of Southern culture.

When I ran upon Josephine Habersham's diary in the Southern Historical Collection at the University of North Carolina it was my intention to edit it for óne of the historical journals, but not finding in it an answer to the important questions of the fate of the Habersham soldier boys nor of the destiny of the Southern aristocracy which this family represents I determined to carry the story to its conclusion. This was made possible by the discovery of Josephine's Letter Book which is in the possession of her great-granddaughter, Josephine Crisfield (Mrs. William Spencer) Connerat of Savannah. Some use is made, too, of the diary of Anna, Josephine's daughter, who, at the age of fifteen in 1864, tells very effectively of the impact of war's tragedy upon her home. Her son, the late George Noble Jones, published 100 copies of his mother's diary (*Journal of Anna Wylly Habersham*, Savannah, 1926, 20 pp.). The original remains in the possession of his family. Anna's son and daughters, Josephine Noble Jones (Mrs. J. A. P. Crisfield) and Mary Savage Jones (Mrs. Clarence G. Anderson), were immediately interested when I approached them with my plan to edit Josephine's diary. I found Mrs. Crisfield and Mrs. Anderson gracious hostesses at Avon, the Vernon River home which had been in the family for a hundred years. Mrs. Crisfield passed away in November, 1953, and George Noble Jones died in December, 1955. Mrs. Anderson continued to help me, especially in the difficult work of establishing family connections, until she, too, died in March, 1958. In addition to Mrs. Anderson, I wish to acknowledge my thanks, also, to Annie Simkins (Mrs. Samuel Fair) Marshall and Anna Colquitt (Mrs. G. L. C.) Hunter, of Savannah; Harriet R. Colquitt, of Bluffton, South Carolina; and Joseph Clay Habersham Colquitt, of Washington, D. C., for permission to publish their grandmother's diary.

I wish to thank Dr. James W. Patton, Director of the Southern Historical Collection, for his assistance and for sending me a microfilm copy of the diary by which my daughter, Janet Paul, and I proofed the typescript. Mrs. Crisfield gave the original document to the Southern Historical Collection in March, 1947. It is a volume $5\frac{1}{2}$ by 9 inches and is about $\frac{1}{4}$ inch thick, containing 104 pages. It has a cover of thin cardboard, black on the outside. The paper, a very pale blue with faint lines running through the length rather than the width of the book, appears to have

PREFACE   xi

been sewed into the cover by hand. Apparently, Mrs. Habersham used a record book of marine risks which belonged to her husband, the junior partner of R. Habersham & Son, for on the paper glued on the front cover the firm name is marked through and there remains the line, "Mutual Safety Insurance Co." Above and below this line she has written:

Private Diary
Josephine C. Habersham
Avon, June 1863.

The writing runs parallel with the lines so that while the reader holds the volume like an ordinary book to read the notation on the cover, he must turn it sidewise to read the diary itself.

Josephine's Letter Book, which is owned by Mrs. Connerat, has a brown leather cover. A half-inch gold flowered border and lines forming a rectangle in the center appear on front and back. In the rectangle on the front, printed in gold block letters, are the words "Savannah Whist Club." Obviously, it was started as a record book of this club for near the front appear the "Rules of the Whist Club." But Josephine converted it into a letter book and depository of Shakespearean and other quotations—including some original poetry. She turned the book upside down and numbered the pages from one to 260. The volume is 7½ by 10 inches and about ¾ of an inch thick.

Josephine's penmanship is not what one would call beautiful. It does not have the sharpness and symmetry one might expect of a pupil of Madame Chégaré, her New York teacher, but the letters are open and consistently well formed so that one becomes accustomed to reading it after a little practice.

I have tried faithfully to present the diary as Josephine wrote it, following her spelling and capitalization in almost every instance, italicizing the words she underlined for emphasis, and holding to many of her dashes and incomplete sentences. However, in order to make the meaning clear and to facilitate the reading I have lowered the letters which she raised above the line, spelled out the abbreviations, eliminated scores of dashes, and changed her punctuation where clarity demanded it.

In order to conserve space, Josephine hardly ever broke the writing, even to start a new paragraph. Nevertheless, the diary falls naturally into chapters that fit into the calendar months from June through October. I have given titles to these chapters which seem to me appropriate—and I believe Josephine would have approved my choices.

Next to Mrs. Anderson, I am indebted to Lilla M. Hawes, Director of the Georgia Historical Society, Hodgson Hall, Savannah, Georgia. She has been extremely helpful in research problems. My thanks, too, to Walter Hartridge, President of the Georgia Historical Society, for keeping me informed on Savannah history. Dr. Benjamin W. Griffith, Jr., Professor of English at Mercer University, was very helpful with suggestions as to literary style. I am deeply indebted to him. I sincerely thank Dr. E. Merton Coulter, Department of History of the University of Georgia, for his valuable suggestions.

The art work of William Etsel Snowden, Jr., of Atlanta, has been a labor of love that has stretched over many hours in order to make the sketches authentic and in harmony with the atmosphere of the narrative and in tune with its mood. Lillie Crisfield (Mrs. William T.) Dixon, of Worten, Maryland, along with Mrs. Anderson, furnished photographs and daguerreotypes from which some of the sketches were made. The late Margaret Schley Rockwell Snowden, wife of the artist and great-granddaughter of Josephine through Josephine's son Robert, made valuable suggestions and checked the manuscript for errors.

It is not possible to name everyone who has assisted me in this work, but in addition to those already named, I wish to mention the following: Lillian Henderson, Director of the (Georgia) Confederate Pension and Record Department;

F. M. Hutson of the South Carolina Department of Archives; J. M. Edelstein, Reference Librarian, Library of Congress; Georgia Benedict, Albany, New York; Margaret Davis Cate, Sea Island, Georgia; Edmond Keith, Atlanta, Georgia; and Mrs. Mark Cooper, Rome, Georgia. My sincere thanks, also, to my colleagues at Mercer University — Dean Malcolm Lester, Major James E. Davis, Dr. David W. Johnston, Charles H. Stone, and Anne LeConte McKay; and three of my students — James T. Hatcher, Jr., Sylvia Cameron, and Osteen Bland.

I make my final word of appreciation to Ralph H. Stephens, Director of the University of Georgia Press, whose skill transformed my manuscript into this book.

Spencer B. King, Jr.

Macon, Georgia
Summer, 1958

A thousand rills in soft harmonious flow
Run trickling through the main,
And join in voices sweet and low
Bright Vernon's gorgeous train.
—William Waring Habersham,
"Sunset on Vernon River"

AVON

THIS is the story of Avon, the William Neyle Habersham summer home at White Bluff about ten miles out from Savannah on the Vernon River, and of the family which lived there. It is told mainly by Josephine Clay Habersham through her little handmade diary kept in the summer and fall of 1863; but her Letter Book and the diary of Anna, her young daughter, help to bring the narrative to its close the following year when Sherman gave Savannah to President Lincoln for a Christmas present. It was there at Avon, or Avon Hall as she sometimes called it, that Josephine and William Neyle and their children and servants found tranquility in escape from the heat and work-a-day world of Savannah. But with all the outward calm of Avon, Josephine could not find real peace, for the war drums were beating loud in the summer of 1863, and, though beginning to grow deaf, she could hear them in her heart.

Josephine was a lover of fine music and good literature. Beethoven and Mozart were her favorite composers, and Shakespeare and Tennyson her favorite authors. She often wrote quotations from Shakespeare in her diary—and very accurate quotations they were, too. It was not by mere chance, then, that she chose the bard's own river name for the summer home which her husband bought for her in 1854. There is uncertainty as to the origin of the name of Vernon River. Some say it bears the name of James Vernon, a member of the first Board of Trustees of the colony; others say it perpetuates the memory of Admiral Edward Vernon, who helped Oglethrope drive the Spaniards from Georgia.

The front of the house, facing the river, has about the same appearance it had when William Neyle Habersham bought it; but the opposite side, which one approaches on the drive up the White Bluff road from Savannah, has had added to it the white columns that once adorned the interior of the house of his father, Robert Habersham. An evergreen hedge extends across the wide front lawn at Avon. Beyond the hedge the lawn slopes gradually down to the river and the boat landing. To the sides and in the rear of the house are some of the large live oaks, dripping with gray moss, which shaded the children at play in those busy and sometimes momentous days when Josephine kept her diary.

William Neyle Habersham married his cousin Josephine Clay Habersham in 1840 and fourteen years later bought the Vernon River house which Josephine named Avon Hall. The Reverend Benjamin Burroughs, pastor of the White Bluff Presbyterian Church, had owned the house, but after the tragic death of their little daughter Laura, the Burroughs family moved away. The house is situated on the west bank of the Vernon River at White Bluff just above Rose Dhu. At the time of the diary Patrick Houstoun lived at Rose Dhu. A lineal descendant of old Sir Patrick Houstoun of colonial days, Patrick, like his ancestor, was "somewhat a diamond in the rough,"[1] but good hearted. The boys were attracted to his place, especially in watermelon season, for Patrick grew the finest watermelons in the county. The White Bluff settlement was known as Vernonburg in colonial days, and the name has survived to this day. The first settlers were German-Swiss; and two of these families, the Nungezers and the Kieffers, continued to live there into the twentieth century.[2] At the bend of the river, just below Avon and in sight of the house, is the village of Montgomery, named for General Richard Montgomery, a native of Ireland, who

1. Charles H. Olmstead, "Reminiscences." Georgia Historical Society, Hodgson Hall, Savannah, Ga.
2. See George Noble Jones, "The Vernon River," *Georgia Review*, IV, 1 (Spring, 1950), pp. 89-96.

fell at Quebec on December 13, 1775, fighting for American freedom. At the next bend is Beaulieu, which William Stephens, Secretary of the Georgia colony, called "Bewlie" —a corruption of the original spelling of his ancestral estate in England. John Schley owned the plantation when Josephine wrote her diary. After the war Schley sold most of the plantation, some to Charles H. Olmstead, some to Alfred L. Hartridge, and some to others. There was good fishing at 'Possum Island—or Rotten 'Possum, as it was originally named—just off Beaulieu point. Just beyond Beaulieu is Burnside Island, which was owned by the McAlpin and Schley families. The last highland on the Vernon River as it flows eastward into Ossabaw Sound is Green Island. It was originally granted to the Delegal family, but was soon after acquired by the Stiles family. The Kings of Barrington Hall usually spent the summers on Green Island. Robert E. Lee erected a battery at Beaulieu in 1861 as a part of the fortification of the Savannah area.[3] At Thunderbolt, about three miles east of Yamacraw Bluff, another battery was built to further augment the protection given by Fort Pulaski. Three miles east of Avon, beyond the marshes and on the Skidaway Narrows, is Wormsloe, on the Isle of Hope, which was the estate of Noble Jones. Wormsloe is still, after two hundred years, owned by the family. Its present mistress is Elfrida De Renne Barrow (Mrs. Craig Barrow), the great-great-great-granddaughter of the original owner. The ruins of Fort Wimberly are still to be seen on the same site where Jones Fort had stood as a defense against the Spaniards during the eighteenth-century War of Jenkins' Ear. A short distance southwest of Avon is Coffee Bluff at the Point where Forest River empties into the Little Ogeechee. The Habersham family and their friends often fished at Coffee Bluff. Genesis Point is farther down, on the Big Ogeechee, where Fort McAllister stood.

3. See Robert Walker Groves, "Beaulieu Plantation," *Georgia Historical Quarterly*, XXXVII (Sept., 1953), pp. 200-209. General Pulaski welcomed Count d'Estaing there when he made his unsuccessful attempt in 1779 to drive the British out of Savannah.

Robert Bolton owned the land from the White Bluff Church to the Kollock place at the nine-mile turn in the White Bluff road. Next to it was the Johnston place, and just beyond was the Adams and Wylly place where Josephine's parents lived. They owned all the land from the Vernon River, where the house stood, to the Little Ogeechee River, and sent cotton to Savannah over the Savannah-Ogeechee canal. No one seems to know how old the house was when William Neyle Habersham bought it. Its history probably goes back to the end of the eighteenth century. Colonel Charles H. Olmstead, who lived in the house as a boy while attending the Reverend Burroughs' School in 1848, thought it probably was built by Robert Bolton in 1799. The Reverend Burroughs, a graduate of Princeton, taught in his own home. Charles Olmstead, along with the two Burroughs boys and others, was invited to live with the Burroughs family in order to study under this minister schoolmaster. The character of the place was early formed, as can be seen from the reminiscences of Colonel Olmstead. The Colonel, by the way, was the officer who had the unpleasant duty of surrendering Fort Pulaski to the Federal forces after a thirty-hour bombardment on April 11, 1862.

Olmstead found the Burroughs place to be "really a small plantation," though the only things sent to market were the products of the dairy. The fields and gardens provided nearly everything that was needed for the support of the family. There were corn, potatoes, peas, millet, sugar cane, and vegetables of all kinds, melons, and fruit in abundance. A well-filled poultry yard supplied meat, and the river yielded up tasty sea food. A fine herd of cows stocked the dairy. In the rear of the house was a large yard in which there "were many grand old pine trees that must have been part of the virgin forest."[4] On each side of the house were the various farm buildings, the barns, stables, carriage houses, and sugar mill. And beyond was the woodland, and in the

4. Olmstead, "Reminiscences."

shade of the trees were the Negro quarters.

Tragedy fell upon the Burroughs home, as it would fall, again and again, upon Avon. Josephine's diary is filled with joy and happiness, but it also has much sorrow in it. During that war-summer and fall of 1863 Avon was the scene of much sadness; but the curse of pain and sadness had already fallen upon it before William Neyle bought it. Even more sorrow would fill the hearts of Josephine and her family as memories of happier days lingered with them in summers to come. The greatest tragedy to come to the Burroughs family was the death of their little daughter Laura. This is the way Olmstead tells the story: "Little Laura was the pet of the household, the last for whom a tragic fate could have been anticipated. Her parents had driven out to visit some of the church people who lived out on the Montgomery Cross Roads, and in their absence the little girls had gone by permission to see the Creamer children whose home was on the upper reach of the river. Just there the Bluff had been badly washed and was almost perpendicular. At its foot was a broad stretch of beautiful sandy beach and there the children went to play. While digging houses in the sand the bluff suddenly caved and fell upon them, covering several of them more or less. Rosa and Laura were entirely out of sight. The former was near the surface, however, and managing to get one hand out, was rescued by Eban Williams and the other children, but poor little Laura could not be found by them and when help arrived she was quite dead."[5]

Some of the Presbyterian atmosphere around the house was dispelled when the Reverend Burroughs moved away and the house changed ownership, for the Habershams were Episcopalians. Josephine herself grew up in the Presbyterian faith and was a member of the Independent Presbyterian Church of Savannah; but she often worshiped with her family at Christ Church, and they went with her to the White Bluff Presbyterian Church while they lived at Avon.

5. *Ibid.*

But most of the ghosts in the house since 1854 have been Episcopal spirits.

The year in which Neyle bought the house was the time of a great hurricane, but the house withstood that storm and continued through the years to weather the storms. Wind and waves have washed away the bluff at Avon Hall, and many of the big trees on the green, sloping lawn are gone; but the new, well-kept lawn has an abundance of shrubbery now, and the big trees in the rear of the house and farther up the river with their lacy moss make an appropriate frame for the three-story home with its banistered porches reaching completely across the front on the first two floor levels. Nearly a hundred years ago Neyle imported from France some of the first camellia plants in the Savannah area. These he planted in his gardens in town and at Avon. They are now large trees, blooming from October to April. At Avon, and down the Vernon River at Rose Dhu on the opposite bank at Montgomery and Beaulieu, can be seen hedges of green cassena with their bright red berries, cherry laurel and azaleas, dark green pittosporum with its sweet-smelling waxy flowers, the fragrant tea olive, pomegranate, Japanese plum, and opoponax, each dressing itself in blooms or foliage in its season and reaching full glory in summer as the mimosa, oleanders, crape myrtles, and altheas add their gay colors.

Family portraits by such well-known artists as Rembrandt Peale, Jeremiah Theus, and George Peter Alexander Healy have adorned the walls at Avon. Though some have been distributed to various members of the family recently, two fine portraits by Theus, the Charleston painter, one of James Habersham, the original settler, and the other of Thomas Savage, still may be seen among the paintings that line the walls. There is a Bompiani of Sarah Campbell—sister of George Fenwick Jones—painted in Rome. She was known as "Miss Noble Jones." There is a beautiful rosewood grand piano, on which Josephine played in her late years, and other furniture and odds and ends, all of which are dear to those who live today to cherish them. The house is filled with treasures and memories. But those who remember are growing fewer. Those who played about the skirts of Josephine in 1863 and those who left to go off to war now lie in well-marked and beautiful graves in the quiet resting places at Laurel Grove and Bonaventure cemeteries. William Neyle-- Josephine called him "Neyle"—and his wife are buried in Laurel Grove. So are Joseph Clay and William Neyle, Jr., two of the soldier boys. In fact, most of the children are buried in Laurel Grove; and great oaks wearing gray mossy mourning veils shade their graves from the hot Georgia sun.

To understand who Josephine and her children and kin were it is necessary to go back to the founding days of the Georgia colony. There we find James Habersham, son of James Habersham, of Beverley, Yorkshire, England, coming to assist George Whitefield at the Bethesda orphanage in 1738. His brother Joseph came over with him, but died the next year. Little is known of Joseph Habersham except that William Stephens recorded in his *Journal* how he wandered into the marsh land of the Vernon River and was lost for two days. James Habersham married Mary Bolton. They had three sons, James, Joseph, and John. The elder James, a staunch Tory, died in 1775, having two years before, as acting governor of Georgia, dissolved the rebellious assembly. His three sons, however, were patriots. James, the eldest son, had five children, one of whom was Esther, the mother of Bishop Stephen Elliott, first Episcopal bishop in Georgia. "Cousin Stephen" baptized all but two of Josephine's children.[6] John, the youngest son, was a major in the Continental Army.[7] He married Ann Sarah Camber. Josephine named her last child Edward Camber—he is "Cherry Cheeks" of the diary. John was the father of Doctor Joseph Clay Habersham, who married Ann Wylly Adams. Josephine

6. Josephine Clay Habersham, Letter Book, in possession of her great-granddaughter, Josephine Crisfield (Mrs. William Spencer Connerat, Savannah, Ga.). Hereafter cited Letter Book.
7. See C. C. Jones, Jr., *Biographical Sketch of the Honorable Major John Habersham* (Cambridge [1886]), p. [5].

was their child, born on January 14, 1821. One of her brothers was also named Joseph Clay. One needs to be alert to avoid confusing Josephine's father, brother, and son. However, when she is speaking of her son he is usually "dear Joseph Clay." Joseph Habersham, the second son, rose from the rank of major to colonel in the Continental Army. It was he who boldly arrested Sir James Wright, the Royal Governor, by order of the Council of Safety. President Washington made him Postmaster General of the United States. Joseph married Isabella Rae. Their son, Robert, married three times. His first wife was Mary O'Brien and his third was Mary Butler Habersham, his first cousin. William Neyle was Robert's son by his second wife, Elizabeth Neyle. Neyle's sister, Isabella, died young, but he had several half brothers and sisters. The paternal grandfathers of Neyle and Josephine were brothers, making them second cousins.[8]

A story told by George Noble Jones, Josephine's grandson, illustrates the friendly repartee that was often heard at Avon. One day while lunch was being served on the piazza overlooking the Vernon River, Josephine's mother, Ann Wylly Adams Habersham, whose home was farther down the river, boasted that the sea breezes were stronger at her place—that often the silver was blown off the table. Neyle, her son-in-law, quickly replied: "But, Mother Ann, that happened because the Adams silver is so much lighter than the Habersham silver."[9]

Josephine was one of seven children of Dr. Joseph Clay Habersham and Ann Wylly Adams. One brother, Joseph Clay, Jr., already mentioned, married Mary Anna Stiles. Like his father before him, he was a physician. A sister, Anna Wylly, married Charles Barrington King, who, at the time of the diary, was the minister at White Bluff Presbyterian Church. Charles, a graduate of Princeton, was the oldest son

---

8. Mrs. Clarence Anderson. Compare Joseph Gaston Baille Bulloch, *A History and Genealogy of the Habersham and Other Families* (Columbia, S. C., 1901).
9. Quoted in *Georgia Review*, IV, 1 (Spring, 1950), p. 92.

of Barrington King and Catherine Margaret Nephew of Barrington Hall, Roswell, Georgia. Josephine records in her diary the death of Charles' brother, Captain Thomas King, killed at Chickamauga. Another sister was Mary Ann. She married Joseph Washburn. Mr. Washburn's tombstone is a four-sided one. On one side is his name, and on the other three sides are the names of his three wives. Mary Ann was his third wife. She was very kind to her sisters and brothers. A wonderful seamstress, "she often wished for a needle that would jump up and down by itself for ruffles and tucks."[10] Mary Ann was the sister for whom Josephine is found weeping as the diary begins. Another brother, William Waring, married Johanna Wade. He loved nature and expressed that love in poetry. An example is his poem, "Sunset on the Vernon River," written in 1892 at Montgomery, on the point of land down the river from White Bluff.

> With mild effulgence sinks the Orb of Day,
> Where nature reigns supreme;
> Bathing with lustre pure and bright as May,
> This beauteous inland stream;
> A thousand rills in soft harmonious flow
> Run trickling through the main,
> And join in voices sweet and low
> Bright Vernon's gorgeous train.
>
> The neighboring Isles, in all their lustrous green
> Shine brightly in the sunset glow;
> Playing amidst the rippling waves, whose sheen
> Like Childhood's laughter, is brighter as they go
> Towards the boundless sea;
> Marking their course, like Mermaids free,
> In acts of revelry and glee.[11]

Josephine's third brother, John Bolton, lived in Brunswick and married Frances Hazlehurst. Josephine's other sister was Frances, or Fanny, the "beauty of the family."[12] She married

10. Josephine Jones (Mrs. J. A. P. Crisfield), undated note to her daughter, Josephine Crisfield (Mrs. William Spencer Connerat), Savannah, Ga.
11. In the possession of Mrs. William Spencer Connerat, Savannah, Ga.
12. George Noble Jones, Savannah, Ga., grandson of Josephine, Anna's son. He died in December, 1955.

Louis Manigault of Charleston, of an honored French Huguenot family. Manigault was in correspondence with Josephine before he began to court Frances. He wrote his first letter in French and she replied in kind. Then he used Italian as his language medium for his second letter, and she answered in that language. His third letter was written in German. To his amazement, Josephine answered in German. He thought he had caught her with his next letter, which was in Chinese, but she was equal to him in cleverness if not in linguistics. She sent him a letter composed of the Chinese symbols copied from a tea caddy! Louis and Frances gave their baby her aunt's name, and Josephine was very fond of her namesake. Louis had fallen violently in love with Frances and manifested it with all the ardor of his warm French blood. After their marriage he took time out on a business trip to Savannah in December, 1863, to visit again his "Old Courting Ground."[13] A particular cedar tree held secrets that only the lovers knew. That cedar went down the bluff in a storm many years ago, but "branches from its roots continue to come out among the other bushes."[14]

William Neyle Habersham was born on July 25, 1817. He was a rice merchant operating a steam rice mill on the Savannah River. On the death of his father he became the head of the Habersham firm, founded in 1744, that owned a fleet of ships carrying Georgia products across the Atlantic and returning "in ballast with the wines of Spain and Madeira."[15] Commerce had been a part of the life of the Habershams from the beginning, when James, the founder of the family in Georgia, joined Francis Harris in establishing an early commercial house in the colony and shipped the first

13. Louis Manigault, Diary. This diary and letter book is in the possession of Manigault's great-granddaughter, Mrs. Alan B. Northington, Macon, Ga. See *Georgia Historical Quarterly*, XXXVIII (March, 1954), pp. 82-84.
14. Mrs. J. A. P. Crisfield. Mrs. Crisfield died in November, 1953.
15. Malcolm Bell, Jr., "The Romantic Wine of Madeira," *Georgia Historical Quarterly*, XXXVIII, 4 (Dec., 1954), p. 333.

bale of cotton from Georgia. Neyle graduated from Harvard at nineteen. An authority on salmon fishing, he was also recognized as a great authority on Madeira wines. The Georgia Society of Cincinnati made him its president. Neyle's grandfather, Joseph, was one of the founders of this fraternity of Continental Army officers.

Like Josephine, Neyle was a lover of music. The flute was his instrument, and it was his custom to play upon it about two hours each day until his death on September 20, 1899. On his tomb in Laurel Grove cemetery is chiseled a flute and three bars of Lowell Mason's familiar hymn, "Nearer, My God, to Thee." Lowell Mason, himself, spent the years 1812-1827 in Savannah. Neyle's flute is preserved at the Georgia Department of Archives and History in Atlanta. Though not so widely known a flutist as Sidney Lanier, Neyle was admired by Cambridge poets and writers for his mastery of the instrument. He had followed his elder brother Robert from the Round Hill School at Northampton to Harvard and while there boarded at the widow Craigie's house. Henry W. Longfellow, then a professor at Harvard, stayed at the same place. Longfellow said of him: "He was a skillful performer on the flute. Like other piping birds he took wing for the rice-fields of the South when the cold weather came, and I remained alone with the widow in her castle."[16] And Thomas Wentworth Higginson describes how, when he was a small boy, he used to leave the door of his little bedroom ajar, when sent to bed at eight o'clock, in order that he might go to sleep to the flute trios of John Dwight, Christopher Pearse Cranch, and William Neyle Habersham.[17] Neyle had Thursday evening musicales in his Savannah home. Felix Lessing, who taught the Habersham girls their piano lessons, often played on these occasions and accompanied such well-known artists as Ole Bull, the Norwegian violinist.

16. Samuel Longfellow, ed., *Life of Henry Wadsworth Longfellow with Extracts from his Journals and Correspondence* (Boston, 1891), I, 264.
17. Thomas Wentworth Higginson, "Cheerful Yesterdays," *Atlantic Monthly*, LXXVIII (Nov., 1896), pp. 589-590.

Hearing became more difficult for Josephine in her later years, but she continued to play the piano and to accompany Neyle as he played the flute. The Negro boys working in the garden were often heard whistling Mozart, Beethoven, and Kuhlau sonatas. Even in the late years of life Josephine would enter into the family concerts; but near the end she had to be content to sit back and listen, with the aid of her ear trumpet, to the violin, flute, and piano trios of her grandchildren. Colonel John Screven wrote of her musical ability in the following words: "She became a charming vocalist and a pianist of such accomplishment that professional artists sought to test her skill, and wondered at her extemporaneous reading of the most difficult compositions, at the quick genius infallible in the modulation of harmonical accompaniments unseen and unheard before, at the consummate execution of this mistress of their own art. Nor did the sad infirmity, which gradually impaired and finally destroyed her sense of sound, arrest her devotion to the art she loved. Her music was in and of the soul, and like Beethoven, deaf even to his own grand symphonies, she continued almost to the last to pour out for the delight of others strains which she herself could hear only with the spiritual ear."[18] After suffering for a long time from a bronchial disorder her tender and noble heart stopped beating on November 6, 1893, at the age of seventy-two years and nine months. She lies beside her husband in Laurel Grove, and on her tomb is engraved a verse which she herself composed:

> I long to end my lifeless dream
> And haste me to that shore
> To meet again—ah! blissful thought!—
> The loved ones gone before![19]

A poem of greater depth and lyrical beauty is "The Star and the Flower," which she wrote in 1861:

18. Eulogy by Col. John Screven, Savannah, Nov. 26, 1893. Printed copy (3 pp.) in the papers of Mrs. Clarence G. Anderson, Savannah, Ga. Mrs. Anderson died in March, 1958.
19. Josephine Habersham's tomb in Laurel Grove Cemetery, Savannah, Ga.

> The flower beheld the star above,
> And longed to reach her airy love!
> But longed in vain! A dew-drop fell
> Into the soft and fragrant cell
> And then the star was imaged there,
> Pure as if dropped from upper air,
> And gliding down from heaven had come
> To find on earth a kindred home!
> Blest was the little flower to bear
> In its own breast a thing so fair!
>
> Ah, longing eye! strain not thy gaze,
> Till blinded by the golden rays
> Of light, too strong for mortal's sight!
> Rest thee on earth! here seek thy fill
> Of beauty, in the pictured scene
> Spread round, of woody hill
> And verdant vale; of Nature's mien
> Swift changing with the passing shade
> Of darkling cloud, and skies that fade
> Too soon from morning's promise fair!
>
> Drink in the beauty round thee lying!
> Take earth, with all its joys—its sighing,
> Its morning promise, vainly fair!
> And trust to find in heaven above
> What fails thee here of light and love!
> Let faith and hope the dew-drops be
> That mirror heaven's light to thee![20]

Of Josephine's twelve children, three were denied the joy of life. Only one of these lived long enough to be christened. Josephine Vernon, whose twin brother was dead at birth (September 26, 1858), lived four months. An infant boy, born September 6, 1860, lived only a few minutes. She must have been reflecting on the loss of these babies when she quotes twice in her diary a passage from Tennyson's "The Grandmother" where the grandmother, having told her little Annie how "the first that ever I bare was dead before he was born," goes on to say, "Shadow and shine is life, little Annie, flower and thorn." Two others died young also.

20. As quoted in Screven, *op. cit.*

They were Josephine Elizabeth, born December 4, 1842, and James Edward—"Jamesie" in the diary—born January 8, 1851. Josephine Elizabeth—"Sissy"—died of pneumonia in Boston in 1852, at the age of ten, when her parents took her there visiting friends of Neyle's Harvard days; and "Jamesie" died in 1857 at the age of seven.

Her first child was Joseph Clay, born on May 23, 1841, the year after her marriage. Josephine was at Robert Habersham's home on Orleans Square at the time. At his birth her soul burst out in a six-stanza poem of joy. It was published over her pen name, "Tallulah," in a little book of sentimental poems printed and sold for the benefit of the Episcopal Orphans' Home in Savannah. This is the last verse:

> Oh! *Well* I love my bonny child;
> Could you his graces see,
> You'd say he was an angel mild,
> Sent down from Heaven to me.[21]

When he became fourteen, Joseph Clay enrolled at St. John's School for boys at Sing Sing (now Ossining), New York. A favorite instructor there was Y. U. Phelps, a classical scholar who taught him Latin and Greek. Josephine cherished a letter from Professor Phelps in which he said her son was "a diligent and faithful student. . . . He has many excellent traits of character and enjoys the love, respect, and confidence of all."[22] Then he went to South Carolina College at Columbia where Professor John LeConte became his good friend and teacher. Another letter cherished by Josephine is one written by Professor LeConte, but it concerns the end of our story.

Joseph Clay enlisted as a private in the volunteer "Savannah Guards" on April 1, 1862. They made up Company B of the 17th Georgia Infantry Battalion, a unit of the Army of Tennessee. On April 22, the next year, he was appointed first lieutenant and made an aide-de-camp to Brigadier-General

---

21. *A Southern Winter-Wreath, Culled for the Motherless* (Cambridge, 1866), p. 24.
22. Letter Book, p. 8.

S. R. Gist; then, on May 1, he was ordered to report to Brigadier-General W. Duncan Smith. This order was followed by many others which sent him into engagements from Charleston to Jackson, Mississippi, to Chickamauga and, finally, to Atlanta. This mounted staff officer was a brave and dashing soldier, causing his mother much anxiety mixed with pride in his exploits. The account of his first baptism of fire in his letter of June 17, written from James Island, Charleston harbor, gave her a vivid picture of what it would be like over and over in battle after battle. The Yankees were pounding the Charleston batteries, and General Smith's new and untried aide was being initiated into the realities of war, seeing dead and dying strewn around: mutilated limbs, headless corpses, dead bodies almost covered with sand, cut to pieces on the ramparts, and lying in the moat.

"Mamma," he wrote, "it was *terrible* to look at . . . I was under severe fire myself, and narrowly escaped a rifle cannon ball which passed over *my saddle*, as I *was mounting* my horse! The *wind* of it almost knocked me down as it whistled by. . . ."[23]

Josephine's anxiety was matched by Joseph Clay's eagerness for action. Writing his mother from Fredericksburg on December 17, he said, "On Thursday last, I was in Richmond, and knowing that a battle was expected, I came on here. I could not obtain a pass as I did not belong to the 'Army of the Potomac,' but being determined to come, borrowed one. After difficulties, I arrived in time, and volunteered with the Pulaski Guards, Captain John Read, of Savannah [commanding]. The Battery really did service—slaughtering the Yankees at every shot. General [Stonewall] Jackson on the right prevented our being flanked, and repulsed the enemy every time. I am on the left, in Longstreet's Corps, just in front of Fredericksburg. On Saturday the ground in front of us was literally covered with the enemy's

---

23. Letter Book, p. 224. This is the way Josephine copied the letter. The underlining of words is typical of her.

dead. . . . General Cobb was killed. . . ."[24] And the letter goes on, but this is enough to show how the brave, even cocky, soldier reported his experience in a great battle that resulted in a Confederate victory. He would see more victories in Mississippi, Tennessee, and Georgia, as he galloped his horse to and fro in the thick of battle; but he would also see battles lost before the war was over.

William Neyle, who carried his father's name, but whom Josephine called "Willie," was three years younger than Joe Clay but old enough to go to war, having been born on May 12, 1844. On the eve of the war Willie was a student in a Presbyterian academy at Bloomfield, New Jersey.[25] Apparently, he did not get the thrill of battle that his officer-brother enjoyed. He enlisted as a private in December, 1861, but got a discharge, furnishing W. T. Hannan as a substitute. Later he served on the Confederate cruiser *Nashville*, or *Rattlesnake*,[26] which ran the blockade into Savannah in July, 1862.[27] Then, on August 13, 1862, he joined the "Savannah Cadets," which became Company F, 54th Georgia Infantry.[28]

The third son was Robert Beverley, born on August 30, 1846. He was named for his father's half-brother. "Uncle Robert" was quite a gay young blade when a student at Harvard, as his diary shows.[29] Robert became seventeen during the summer of 1863, and he too saw service. He was in the Confederate Signal Corps Service, stationed at Genesis Point, below Fort McAllister on the Ogeechee River. After the war Robert became a student at the University of Heidelberg. He later married Margaret Cunningham Schley; then,

24. Letter Book, p. 226. This was Thomas R. R. Cobb of Athens, a leader in the secession movement and in the formation of the Confederacy at Montgomery, Ala.
25. Letter from Willie, Dec. 6, 1860. Letter Book, p. 217.
26. Joseph Clay to his mother, Feb. 2, 1863; Letter Book, p. 230.
27. Clement A. Evans, ed., *Confederate Military History* (Atlanta, 1899, 12 vols.), VI, 102, 203. The *Nashville* was the first commissioned armed cruiser of the Confederacy.
28. Georgia Confederate Pension and Record Department, Atlanta Georgia.
29. This diary is in the Georgia Historical Society Collection, Hodgson Hall, Savannah, Ga.

two years after her death, and at Margaret's own request, he married Georgia Maria, her sister. Robert was associated with his father in the Habersham firm located on Bay Street.

Next after Robert came Anna Wylly, born February 4, 1849; she was fourteen years of age in the summer of 1863. Anna rejected the suit of Johnnie Scharf,[30] of Baltimore, the following summer. Johnnie was in the Confederate Navy and stationed at the time on the *Water Witch*. After the war Scharf became the historian of the Confederate Navy. Anna later married George Fenwick Jones. He was the son of George Noble Jones and Mary Savage Nuttall; George Noble was the son of Noble Wymberley Jones and Sarah Campbell. Thus, in Anna's marriage were united two of Georgia's most illustrious families.[31]

Elizabeth Matilda, called "Lilla," was born on January 25, 1853; and Mary Isabella, called "Mary Belle" as a child and later "Mabelle," was born on March 27, 1854. These were Josephine's "little girls," ten and nine respectively. When Lilla grew up she married Walter Wellborn Colquitt, brother of Governor Alfred H. Colquitt; Mary Belle married William D. Simkins of an old Revolutionary family of South Carolina.

Edward Elliott Camber—"Cherry Cheeks"—was born on August 11, 1862, and was only ten months old as the diary opens. He died in the midst of World War I, when all Americans were "Yankees," united in a common cause. Edward attended the University of the South at Sewanee, Tennessee. He never married, but spent most of his life on the Atlantic as a purser with the Ocean Steamship Company, operating between Savannah, New York, and Boston.

30. Anna tells the story of this teen-age romance with John Thomas Scharf in her diary of 1864. A limited edition of this diary was published by her son, George Noble Jones, *Journal of Anna Wylly Habersham, 1864* (Savannah, 1926). Anna's other children were Josephine Noble and Mary Savage.
31. The original spelling of "Wimberly" was changed to "Wymberley"; then, later, on January 12, 1866 the name "De Renne" was legally adopted by George Wymberley Jones. See E. Merton Coulter, *Wormsloe* (Athens, Ga., 1955), p. 215; cf. Bulloch, *op. cit.*, p. 22.

Throughout the diary runs the anguish caused by the fear that tragedy of war might be brought home to her own heart. Josephine saw that fear in the eyes of so many of her friends, and she saw helpless resignation on the countenance of others who had already experienced the loss of a loved one fallen in battle. Another dominant note in the diary is the love of good living—music, poetry, the magazines and books popular in her day, especially the English reviews. Long hours were spent in the careful supervision of the garden with its many flowers; but the harmony of gracious living was disrupted almost daily by the discord of fear and hate engendered by war. Josephine was anxious about her young daughters, too, hoping they would grow into fine ladies, and even during the summer months when school was out she heard "the little girls their lessons." She had had good schooling herself. After attending the Reverend George White's Academy in Savannah, she attended Madame Chégaré's French School in New York. George White had awarded her a "Premium" for excelling her class in spelling. After she grew old and very deaf she continued to hear, with the aid of her ear trumpet, the lessons of her grandchildren. Sometimes they would play tricks on her. Anna's Josephine was very adept at French, while some of her little cousins were negligent about getting up their lessons. Anna's Josephine would hide behind the door and coach her cousin while grandma Josephine, beaming with pride, would praise the "bright little pupil" who recited her French so well.

The spiritual depth of the woman is seen in her diary. She had a faith sufficient to sustain her in the anxious hours and strong enough to fortify her against the sorrows of 1863 and to give her the strength to bear the great tragedy of the following summer. Josephine's diary ends on Communion Sunday, November 1, 1863, but Anna's diary and Joseph Clay's and Willie's letters and letters about them, copied by Josephine in her Letter Book, make possible the last chapter in which the receding tide at war's end sweeps away the family name of Habersham.

HABERSHAM

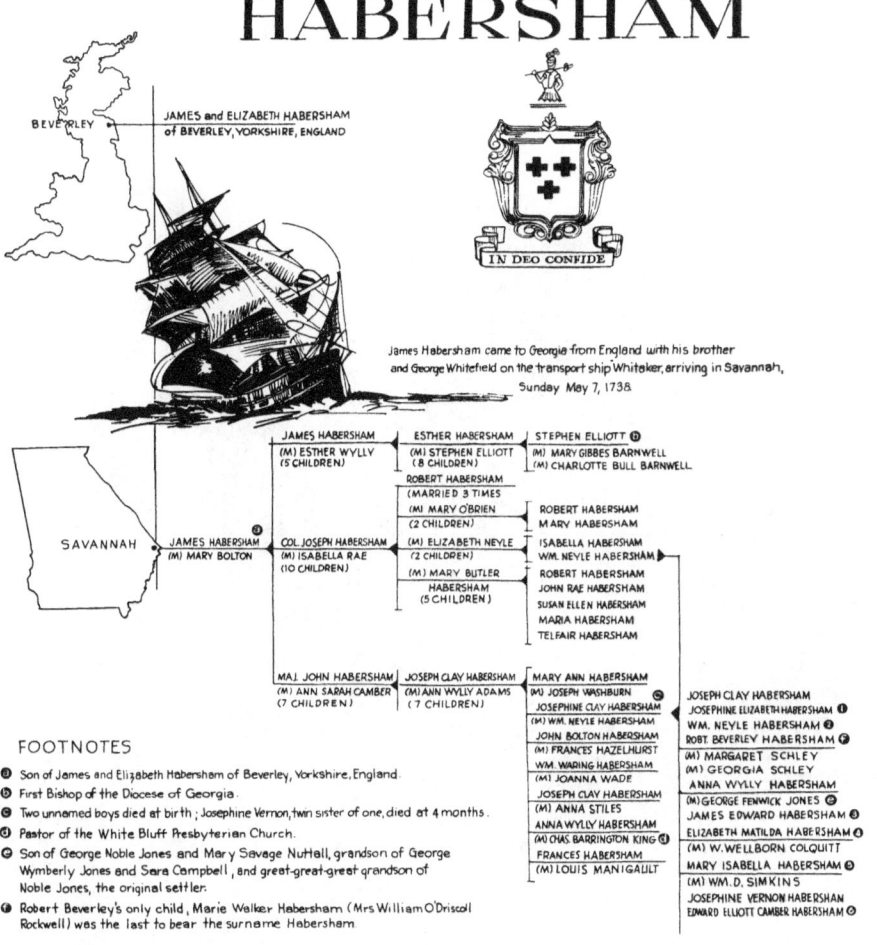

JAMES and ELIZABETH HABERSHAM of BEVERLEY, YORKSHIRE, ENGLAND

BEVERLEY

IN DEO CONFIDE

James Habersham came to Georgia from England with his brother and George Whitefield on the transport ship Whitaker, arriving in Savannah, Sunday May 7, 1738.

SAVANNAH

JAMES HABERSHAM
(M) MARY BOLTON

JAMES HABERSHAM
(M) ESTHER WYLLY
(5 CHILDREN)

ESTHER HABERSHAM
(M) STEPHEN ELLIOTT
(8 CHILDREN)

STEPHEN ELLIOTT ⓑ
(M) MARY GIBBES BARNWELL
(M) CHARLOTTE BULL BARNWELL

ROBERT HABERSHAM
(MARRIED 3 TIMES
(M) MARY O'BRIEN
(2 CHILDREN)

ROBERT HABERSHAM
MARY HABERSHAM

COL. JOSEPH HABERSHAM ⓐ
(M) ISABELLA RAE
(10 CHILDREN)

(M) ELIZABETH NEYLE
(2 CHILDREN)

ISABELLA HABERSHAM
WM. NEYLE HABERSHAM

(M) MARY BUTLER
HABERSHAM
(5 CHILDREN)

ROBERT HABERSHAM
JOHN RAE HABERSHAM
SUSAN ELLEN HABERSHAM
MARIA HABERSHAM
TELFAIR HABERSHAM

MAJ. JOHN HABERSHAM
(M) ANN SARAH CAMBER
(7 CHILDREN)

JOSEPH CLAY HABERSHAM
(M) ANN WYLLY ADAMS
(7 CHILDREN)

MARY ANN HABERSHAM
(M) JOSEPH WASHBURN ⓒ
JOSEPHINE CLAY HABERSHAM
(M) WM. NEYLE HABERSHAM
JOHN BOLTON HABERSHAM
(M) FRANCES HAZELHURST
WM. WARING HABERSHAM
(M) JOANNA WADE
JOSEPH CLAY HABERSHAM
(M) ANNA STILES
ANNA WYLLY HABERSHAM
(M) CHAS. BARRINGTON KING ⓓ
FRANCES HABERSHAM
(M) LOUIS MANIGAULT

JOSEPH CLAY HABERSHAM
JOSEPHINE ELIZABETH HABERSHAM ❶
WM. NEYLE HABERSHAM ❸
ROBT. BEVERLEY HABERSHAM ❹
(M) MARGARET SCHLEY
(M) GEORGIA SCHLEY
ANNA WYLLY HABERSHAM
(M) GEORGE FENWICK JONES ⓖ
JAMES EDWARD HABERSHAM ❷
ELIZABETH MATILDA HABERSHAM ❹
(M) W. WELLBORN COLQUITT
MARY ISABELLA HABERSHAM ❺
(M) WM. D. SIMKINS
JOSEPHINE VERNON HABERSHAM
EDWARD ELLIOTT CAMBER HABERSHAM ⓖ

FOOTNOTES

ⓐ Son of James and Elizabeth Habersham of Beverley, Yorkshire, England.
ⓑ First Bishop of the Diocese of Georgia.
ⓒ Two unnamed boys died at birth; Josephine Vernon, twin sister of one, died at 4 months.
ⓓ Pastor of the White Bluff Presbyterian Church.
ⓔ Son of George Noble Jones and Mary Savage Nuttall, grandson of George Wymberly Jones and Sara Campbell, and great-great-great grandson of Noble Jones, the original settler.
ⓕ Robert Beverley's only child, Marie Walker Habersham (Mrs William O'Driscoll Rockwell) was the last to bear the surname Habersham.

DIARY CHARACTERS SPOKEN OF BY NICKNAMES ❶ SISSY ❷ WILLIE ❸ JAMESIE ❹ LILLA ❺ MARY BELLE ❻ CHERRY CHEEKS

THE HABERSHAM FAMILY AS RELATED TO THE DIARY OF JOSEPHINE CLAY HABERSHAM 1863

"*Leaves have their time to fall
But thou hast all seasons for
thine own, O Death.*"

—Hemans, "The Hour of Death"

THE FORESHADOWING

Life was pleasant at White Bluff in the summer of Josephine's life, and the Vernon River flowed full and free at high tide; but her diary begins in the midst of war, and before it closes summer has faded and she feels the chill of winter as she watches the tide go out. June is a month for boating and fishing and music that can be heard even as far as the boathouse, but the sad overtones of death can be heard too, and the drums in the distance.

Avon, June 17, 1863. Arrived today bringing darling Cherry Cheeks[1] to the place where he was born. He was delighted with everything, dancing out of my arms at the sight of ugly Martin, but pursed up his mouth and then cried out at sight of the river or the Bath-house. Mary had to bring him in, sobbing. I suppose the little fellow thought there was an earth-slide! Neyle,[2] Mary Belle[3] and Lilla[4] were fishing, brought some fish, and had a late but nice dinner. So thankful to meet all well and were it not for the fearful anxieties of this terrible war, our sweet summer home looks as if we might be very happy here. Everything looks clean and neat, verdant and prosperous, even the old fences and Bath-house have been nicely "fixed up."

Yesterday was the anniversary of my beloved Sister's[5] death. Sorry I could not get out to visit her grave. Mama and

1. Edward Elliott Camber, the baby, ten months old.
2. Josephine's husband, William Neyle Habersham.
3. Mary Isabella, called "Mary Belle" or "Mabelle," nine years old.
4. Elizabeth Matilda, called "Lilla," ten years of age.
5. Mary Ann Habersham (Mrs. Joseph Washburn).

Freddie[6] went there. And poor, sweet, pretty Mary Low[7] died this morning! In the bloom of life! I remember her out here, not long ago, so bright and gay and independent, fishing and swimming every day. So young! "Leaves have their time to fall, but thou hast all seasons for thine own, O Death."

June 18, 1863. Neyle went in this morning, and I fervently hope he may bring me my first letter from my dear Joseph Clay[8] since he left for Mississippi. God grant my child health and safety. Got a sweet little note from Anna,[9] enjoying herself at her Grandfather's.[10]

No news today from Vicksburg. Yesterday's papers confirm the report of the capture of the *Atlanta* (*Fingal.*)[11] Oh! how provoking! In Ossabaw Sound,[12] not so very far from us, now! Lilla and Mary Belle all dressed up in long dresses, headdresses, fans, etc., "playing lady." Baby is calling out for Papa all this afternoon. Everything very comfortable and nice now. As soon as I get my Bureau I shall be "quite fixed up."

Night. Thank God for a delightful letter from dear

6. Freddie Wade, step-daughter of Mrs. Washburn.
7. Mary Stiles. She married Andrew Low, and was the mother of Willie Low who married Juliette Gordon, founder of the Girl Scouts. Andrew Low was a British cotton merchant. The Low house, which Andrew built, is now owned by the Georgia Society of the Colonial Dames of America and serves as their headquarters.
8. Joseph Clay Habersham enlisted in Co. B, 18th Batt. Ga. Vol. Inf., Army of Tennessee, C. S. A. (Chatham Co.) "Savannah Volunteer Guards." Private, Apr. 1, 1862. Aptd. 1st Lt. and Aide-de-Camp to Brig. Gen. S. R. Gist, Apr. 22, 1862. Aptd. 1st Lt. and Aide-de-Camp, C. S. A. (to rank from Apr. 22, 1862), and ordered to report to Gen. W. D. Smith for duty, May 1, 1862. Confederate Pension and Record Department, State Capitol, Atlanta, Ga. He was again on Gen. Gist's staff later.
9. Anna Wylly Habersham, Josephine's fourteen-year-old daughter. She married George Fenwick Jones.
10. Robert Habersham, Neyle's father.
11. The *Atlanta* was formerly the British ship *Fingal* which the Confederate government bought in September, 1861, and later renamed the *Atlanta.*
12. She was mistaken; it was Warsaw Sound. See report of Commander Webb in *Official Records of the Union and Confederate Navies* (Washington, 1894-1922, 30 vols., 2 series), Ser. I, Vol. XIV, 290-292. Hereafter cited *Official Records, Navy.*

Joseph Clay, dated June 9, Canton [Mississippi] 50 miles from Yazoo City, his place of destination. He had met with Wade Hampton, Jr. Aide of General Joseph Johnston, and had dined with General Joseph Johnston. He is well and happy and writes a most affectionate and interesting letter. Dear Boy, begging me not "to think of him all the time" and to remember that there were thousands of fond Mothers with two or three sons in the Army.

June 19, 1863. Neyle stayed out today, and he, Robert[13] and I went fishing. That is, I shut my eyes to the hook and line business and opened them to the "azure permanence" overhead and a volume of Tennyson in my lap. A brisk rain came up, but I was protected by two Aquascutums, and the breeze was delightful. I made a net, by Neyle's request, for Mr. Higham,[14] and sent by express. He says he is killed by mosquitoes. "No King in Christendom could be better bit," as Falstaff says, than, I suppose, he is.

Have been reading some in Shakespeare today, *Antony and Cleopatra*, and some in Tennyson. Tonight, Mary Belle asked me to read aloud his "May Queen," to every word of which she listened intently.

Wrote to J. C. and Willie[15] (in Augusta) today. Feel much relieved about J. C. He says everything looks bright and clear in Mississippi. General Johnston[16] is confident and

13. Robert Beverley Habersham, Josephine's sixteen-year-old son. Robert reached his seventeenth birthday on Aug. 30 and he, too, entered Confederate service. He was in the Signal Corps Service, stationed at Genesis Point, below Fort McAllister on the Ogeechee River.
14. Thomas Higham, Jr., was from Newport, R. I. His love of literature and music made him a welcome visitor at Avon—when he didn't stay too long. He sold Lapithowly Plantation on the Causton Road to Robert Habersham, Neyle's father, in 1849. Robert changed the name to Deptford. See Record of Deeds, Chatham Co., Savannah Ga.
15. William Neyle Habersham, Jr., Private, Dec. 9, 1861. Discharged. Furnished W. T. Hannan as substitute. Aug. 13, 1862, enlisted as a private in Co. F., 54th Georgia Infantry. Confederate Pension and Record Department, State Capitol, Atlanta, Ga. Willie had served previous to his second enlistment on the Confederate cruiser *Nashville*.
16. General Joseph Eggleston Johnston, of Virginia, a general of ability but overcautious, joined his force with Beauregard to defeat the Federals at Bull Run, attacked them at Seven Pines, failed to successfully unite with Pemberton at Vicksburg, and before being relieved by Hood under order of President Davis, who never liked him, defeated

taking time to organize his Army. Vicksburg still heroically firm and has the means of keeping so. J. C. is near friends, Mallery King,[17] Butler, Hampton, Smith,[18] etc.

Baby had a two hours' play tonight, crowing and laughing so loud as to be heard all over the house, flat on his back, kicking away 'till 10 o'clock.

June 20, 1863. Avon. The anniversary of my beloved Sister's funeral![19] Well do I remember how sadly she was brought back to the home *which should* have been hers only to be laid there, for a night, to be conducted to the tomb! And a wretchedly stormy night it was! With dread-peals and fearful flashes of lightning. Sister Mary[20] stayed with me while Neyle was watching at *her* unconscious side! Sick and miserable as I was I went to the Cemetery. Joseph Clay[21] and I the only very near ones of all her large family, and Ingersoll and Eddie.[22]

Today Willie returned from a very delightful visit to Augusta—looking well and fine. Vicksburg still nobly holds out. What a noble instance of heroic firmness she presents! Last accounts represent "things fair" and Joseph Clay's letter gives a bright idea of everything. Johnston, he says, surely and thoroughly organizing his army, *which* he has divided in several places. J. C. says he has an immense force of Cavalry, 4,000. The papers were filled today with *gratifying* news that Lee was taking his army into Yankeedoodledom![23]

    Sherman at Kennesaw Mountain. Finally, nine days after Appomattox, he surrendered to Sherman near Durham, N. C.
17. Mallery Page King, son of Thomas Butler King, of St. Simons Island. He was named for Garrick Mallery, a prominent attorney of Wilkes-Barre, Pennsylvania, under whom his father had studied law. Mallery managed to get away from war long enough to go to Tebeauville (Waycross) and marry Eugenia Grant.
18. Probably Lee Butler. Hampton was probably Wade Hampton, Jr. Smith cannot be identified.
19. Mary Ann. She had died on June 16, 1862.
20. Neyle's sister, Mrs. William Elliott.
21. This was her brother.
22. Ingersoll and Eddie Washburn were Mary Ann's stepsons. She had no children of her own.
23. Lee had decided to invade the North rather than to send troops west where the Federals were threatening to cut the Confederacy at the Mississippi.

Would it were so! There are reports of intense excitement at the North and fears of the safety of Philadelphia and Harrisburg, etc. God grant that we may be enabled to teach these wretches the bitter lesson of experience in warfare on their own soil!

June 21, 1863. Sunday. Avon. All went to Church[24] but I as I feared the damp for my throat. It *poured* while they were in Church. A quiet Sunday. Played much with dear Baby. He gazed at the rain and turned to me as if to ask an explanation. He gets fatter and heavier every day. The little girls and I sang hymns in the piazza. We miss Anna so much.

Plenty of soldiers pass by every day after dress parade. One man came yesterday to buy a chicken for a sick soldier, but I gave it to him. I am so unused to such things, that I felt as if I were doing a *cruel act,* to put the innocent *live* chicken in the big soldier's power. " 'Tis excellent to have a Giant's strength, 'tis tyrannous to *use* it as a Giant." I've no doubt we were cruel Giants in the chicken's idea!

June 22, 1863. Monday. We are quite a large household, as of old! Mr. Carmichael,[25] child and nurse made themselves visible out of cloaks and blankets, in a pouring rain. Just after, Freddie and Robert. Mr. Carmichael and child were not expected just yet, but we have got things nicely ready for them. Little Mary Belle rejoiced to sleep with Freddie in Grandma's bed. Today I said something about "not much difference between a minute and two minutes," and Lilla said "*a great deal* sometimes. Any how it takes 120 seconds instead of 60." Mary Belle read aloud the May Queen and St. Agnes' Eve, Tennyson. Baby had a royal game of fun in the *piazza* with a napkin ring rolling about. Poor Mary Low!

24. Josephine's family were Episcopalians and belonged to Christ Church in Savannah. They attended the White Bluff Presbyterian Church during their stay at Avon. The White Bluff Church was established in 1743 as "The Congregational Church" or "Meeting House of White Bluff." See *Savannah Evening Press,* Sept. 28, 1956. Josephine herself was a member of the Independent Presbyterian Church in Savannah.
25. William P. Carmichael. He married Eliza Elliott, daughter of Bishop Elliott by his first wife, Mary Gibbes Barnwell.

I think of her constantly. So young and bright and gay! How sudden! "Our little life is rounded with a sleep."

The report is that Lee's advance into Yankee Land is *certain*. Oh! I hope so. I hope they will all be scared to death and learn a little of the misery which they deal to us, with such unsparing hand!

The *Atlanta* supposed to be *grounded*,[26] injured. That's good news! That the enemy will not have her.

Poor Vicksburg bravely firm, at last accounts.

June 23, 1863. Avon. This is our wedding-day. Twenty-three years married! A long happy time to look back upon, yet I can recall many hours of deepest sorrow—years indeed of sorrow! My little Sissy's death! My beloved darling Father's—papa's—my Jamesie's death! What a blow that was to us! But I tried to bear up with my feeble, weak effort of failing humanity; and to bear it *better* than I did our little Sissy's loss when the very sunlight of Heaven was too gay for me! Then I have buried two little infants—the mother's long expectancy over, they died before they were born. The "old grandmother" says in Tennyson, "There lay the sweet little body that never had drawn a breath, and I wept like a child that day, for the babe had fought for its life." I was in a bad way, indeed, with both these little innocents, at their birth—in great peril—but God was good and merciful to me and brought me through with bountiful and remarkable health and strength after such suffering and danger.

26. On June 17 the *Atlanta*, commanded by William A. Webb, started down Warsaw Sound to break the blockade and secure another valuable cargo of munitions from Europe when she was attacked by the *Weehawken*, under the command of Captain John Rodgers, and the *Nahant*, commanded by John Downes. The *Atlanta* ran aground and was the helpless prey of the enemy. Badly crippled by the shots of the *Weehawken*, she hauled down her colors and Commander Webb surrendered to Captain Rodgers. Subsequently, she was sent to the Navy Yard at Philadelphia where she was repaired and put into the service of the United States Navy. Malcolm Maclean, "The Short Cruise of the C. S. S. *Atlanta*," *Georgia Historical Quarterly*, XL, 2 (June, 1956), 130-143. "The United States steamer *Powhatan* arrived in Delaware Bay on Tuesday, having in tow the famous rebel ironclad *Atlanta*," *New York Times*, Sept. 23, 1863.

Then, one of my little twins, Josephine Vernon, that had outlived its little brother, did not for long live in this world of sin but said goodbye in four months—a beautiful little creature, fat and dimpled, and Dr. Joseph Clay[27] said "The most beautiful wax doll he had ever seen." It looked like Robert Beverley, and Lilla. My Joseph Clay said "it had lived just long enough to make us learn to love it, as an angel in Heaven." J. C. was at Columbia College[28] when she died.

Then my precious Sister's death! Cut off in the full bloom and maturity of perfect, lovely womanhood! Good, gentle, pious, sensible, loving, what was she *not* to that family after years of tried faithfulness to her *own*? She was to me, and to Fanny Manigault,[29] the *best* of Sisters. Yet she did for *me* more than for the rest. All the first years of my married life when I was *gay* and thoughtless and inexperienced she was my right hand. Perhaps there never was a more *useful* life than hers, always! "God's ways are mysterious, past finding out." I shall miss her all my life long whether long or short it be.

We went crabbing after dinner—Neyle, Mr. Carmichael and child, Freddie, Lilla, Mary Belle, Robert Beverley[30] and I—a delicious afternoon with pageantry of clouds. I gave my beloved Husband a little present, a gold locket with pretty Daguerres of Lilla and Mary Bell in it. I wrote Joseph Clay and received a very pleasant letter from Mr. Higham, the first I ever received, although I have had to write him several in "fixing up" his wardrobe for him. And had good news of Vicksburg, that the enemy had been again repulsed, with dreadful slaughter, from Vicksburg. All eyes are turned towards Grant and Johnston. God grant that we may soon hear something decisive from Johnston. I fear Grant will have too much time for fortifying himself. Lee, too, will effect something in a few days. Been reading Tennyson lately.

27. Josephine's brother, the family doctor.
28. South Carolina College, now the University of South Carolina. Joseph Clay graduated with the Class of 1861.
29. Frances, Josephine's sister, had married Louis Manigault of Charleston.
30. Robert Beverley, Josephine's son, 16 years of age.

June 24, 1863. Wednesday.[31] Two more arrivals today, Eddie, beaming with the unusual pleasure of a ride out on horseback, and Anna, who had no word for anybody at first, being absorbed by "Cumber,"[32] as Joseph Clay calls him. Baby was overjoyed to see her. He gazed for half a minute and then threw himself against her neck, staying with her, and every now and then a self-offered kiss! She was delighted. They all went rowing after dinner; Baby too, and afterwards Freddie and Robert went to ride on horseback.

June 25, 1863. Thursday. Eddie said goodbye today, gone to school. Mr. Carmichael and child and nurse also off. Mr. Carmichael enjoyed himself, and Andie improved and was very happy. The little girls were very good in playing with him. Mr. Carmichael is very kind and pleasant. Mamma may come out tomorrow. Two delightful long letters from our soldier-boy. So Affectionate. He wrote at half past twelve at night, after a tiresome march. Had crossed the "Big Black."[33] Is with General Gist,[34] on his Staff, happily placed. General Walker[35] offered to make him Chief in Ordnance, but he declined as he wishes to be *on* the field of Battle. They had crossed the Big Black. He was with his good friends, Mallory [*sic*] King, and Lee Butler. *So thankful* to hear from him. He had got a horse, God make my heart truly grateful for all these mercies to me and mine! Repulse at Vicksburg *confirmed.* Grant is badly off since *we* have retaken Millekin's

31. Josephine had erroneously dated it June 25, and continues in error to June 28.
32. Edward Elliott Camber. This, of course, was Edward Camber, "Cherry Cheeks."
33. Grant had defeated Pemberton at Big Black River Bridge on May 17th. J. G. Randall, *Civil War and Reconstruction* (Boston, 1937), 531.
34. Brigadier-General States Rights Gist, of South Carolina. Gist and William H. T. Walker, of Georgia, were both sent to Mississippi to assist Joseph E. Johnston in his "hopeless attempt to save Pemberton" at Jackson and Vicksburg. Walker's brigade consisted of the 25th, 29th, and 30th Georgia regiments, the 1st Georgia battalion Sharpshooters, and Martin's Georgia battery. In Gist's brigade were the 46th Georgia regiment and the 8th Georgia battalion. Gist was later (Nov. 30, 1864) killed at Franklin, Tenn. Evans, *Confederate Military History, op. cit.,* VI, 220; David Duncan Wallace, *History of South Carolina,* III (New York, 1934), 180, 202.

THE FORESHADOWING 29

Bend,³⁶ which prevents his transportations. We hear that the *Atlanta (Fingal)* lies quietly at Fort Pulaski! How provoking!
June 26, 1863. Friday. Wrote my dear Sister Mary Elliott. A most lovely day—one of the real, strong, seabreezes that bring "healing on their wings" blowing. Robert gone in to school, and attends a sociable tonight at Katy Roberts'.³⁷ Anna gone in with Papa for the day to be at the presentation of a gift to Mr. LaCoste³⁸ and Miss Morse. Have been reading all "the Henry's" of Shakespeare lately. How truly beautiful and pathetic are the scenes in Henry the Sixth between Talbot and his son! I hate to find fault with Shakespeare, but do not think he is entirely just to the portrait of Joan of Arc! Surely he denies her the elevation of soul that must have been hers! Prejudice (the English prejudice) against her, must have actuated his pen. Perhaps he tries to exonerate the English from the *shameful barbarity* of her death! But it seems to me he makes her as much too coarse as Schiller makes her too divine and Coleridge as well!
June 27, 1863. Saturday. Wrote to my boy, God bless

35. Major-General Henry Talbot Walker. After the fall of Vicksburg he was ordered back to his native state of Georgia and returned in time to share in the Battle of Chickamauga. In the summer of 1863 he had commanded a brigade under Brig.-Gen. John Gregg, but by October of that year, raised to the rank of Maj.-Gen., he was in command of a division composed of the brigades of Gregg, Gist, and Wilson. General Walker was killed near Atlanta on July 22, 1864—a key date in our story. See *Official Records of the Union and Confederate Armies in the War of Rebellion* (Washington, 1880-1901, 128 books and index. 4 series), Ser. 1, Vol. XXIV pt. 1, pp. 785-787, hereafter cited *Official Records, War.* C. C. Jones, Jr., *A Roster of General Officers, Heads of Departments, Senators, Representatives, Military Organizations, etc.,* etc. in *Confederate Service during the War Between the States* (Richmond, Va., 1876), 20-21. A sketch of General Walker appears in William J. Northen, ed., *Men of Mark in Georgia,* III (Atlanta, 1911), 200-202.
36. Just above Vicksburg on the Mississippi River.
37. Katy Roberts Brown, daughter of Hiram Roberts. Roberts was President of the Merchants & Planters Bank.
38. Henri da la Coste, father of Marie LaCoste. Marie wrote "Somebody's Darling," which was published anonymously in 1864 in *A Southern Winter-Wreath, op. cit.,* 37-39, a poem on the death of a Confederate soldier.

him! Ellen Coleman[39] and sweet children came to spend the day. So glad to see Ellen. She is so fond of and admires Edward so much, and she loved our Jamesie so well—thinks Baby the image of him and Joseph Clay. Mamma came out this evening, and I hope now will stay and bathe and improve with the salt air.

Have read *nothing* today. I got Robert to have his likeness taken today, not very striking. Mamma thinks not at all like him. Freddie thought it was Willie! Strange! Willie stayed in town to attend a meeting of his Regiment. Read some parts of the *Heir of Redclyffe*[40] this evening. Mary Belle reading parts of it.

June 28, 1863. Sunday.[41] A year ago yesterday we came out here, Neyle bringing me, sick and weary and lowspirited, after the death of my dear Sister. Oh! how sad it was! He sent to the Sand Hills[42] for Mary Belle to cheer me up. Joseph Clay was exposed to danger in June, a year ago—on James Island[43] and Willie in the Hussars.[44] We all went to Church. Thank God we were all well, and able to go—leaving little Edward looking very wistfully at us, from the porch. Edgar Guerard[45] dined.

June 29, 1863. Monday. Dinah having a bad hand we have all been playing with Baby. But nothing pleased him so well as to be taken *out* to see the Moos and the bow-wows. Just going to sleep. He has such a winning way, when he wants anything, of putting his lips to be kissed. A heavy thunder storm makes it black as night. I must go in the piazza and watch it coming over the river. The "white horses" dancing about so playfully. A delightful letter from our dear Joseph

---

39. Susan Ellen Habersham, Neyle's half sister, who married William Coleman.
40. Novel by Charlotte Mary Yonge, 1853.
41. This ends the series of erroneous dates. Josephine dated it June 29.
42. The "Sand Hill" was the fashionable section of Augusta.
43. In Charleston harbor.
44. Willie had been discharged, but had enlisted again. This time in Co. F., 54th Georgia Infantry.
45. In 1860 he was a bookkeeper with A. McAlpin & Bros.

THE FORESHADOWING 31

Clay long and interesting and affectionate to his Grandmother Robert H.[46] Such a treat to all of us.

Evening. Mr. Higham, and Major Hartridge[47] came out this evening with Neyle, very unexpectedly, as he always does everything. He was delighted with the place which he says is lovely. It surely *will* be when we can do just a little more to make it so.

June 30, 1863. A lovely day—cool and breezy. Yesterday was a happy day for us, *two* nice long letters from Joseph Clay. While the Army is resting, preparatory to Johnston's *fight* soon to come,[48] he writes often. The last letter for Anna. Today we were sitting on the piazza, Mr. Higham, the girls and I when up through the lawn, drove two fine open barouches, with four white horses, full of people! Willie had brought three Augusta girls, and four young men out to spend the morning. They were all very merry and easy. I showed them that the surprise was not unpleasant. Fortunately, I was nicely dressed in a Spring-like lilac muslin, and not some old country trim! It made all the difference in the world! I could receive them without having to rush off to make myself presentable. We all went crabbing in the sail boat, with awning, and afterwards, a nice lunch, with hot coffee. They had a merry time, and thanked me much. They exclaimed at the idea of my having had 12 children—said I looked about 30![49]

46. Neyle's stepmother, Mary Butler.
47. Major Alfred Lamar Hartridge (1837-1913), C. S. A. He later rose to the rank of colonel. He was the youngest brother of the Honorable Julian Hartridge, member of the Confederate Congress, and later, the United States Congress. Walter Hartridge, Savannah, Ga.; Charles E. Jones, *Georgia in the War, 1861-1865* (Augusta, 1909), 93.
48. Actually Johnston's army was divided from Pemberton's following Grant's victory over Pemberton at Big Black River Bridge in the middle of May. After the Big Black battle Johnston was operating near Jackson and Pemberton was defending Vicksburg. The "fight soon to come," then, was Pemberton's at Vicksburg, where he surrendered his whole force of over 30,000 troops to Grant on July 4. *Official Records, War*, Ser. I, Vol. XXIV, pt. 1, p. 57. Grant claimed 37,000 prisoners. *Ibid.*, 58.
49. She was in her forty-third year.

*"Shadow and shine is life, little Annie,
Flower and thorn."*
—Tennyson, "The Grandmother"

TURNING OF THE TIDE

Josephine saw the "vile" and "wretched" Yankees arriving at a "place of potency and sway" in July. The descriptive adjectives are hers; the quoted phrase is Shakespeare's. The significance of Vicksburg was soon realized, Gettysburg more slowly. Nevertheless, the sun frequently dispelled the shadows.

July 1, 1863. Wednesday. A delightful day. Read a great deal and sewed. Heard the children their lessons and they read to me some of Tennyson's ballads. Mr. Higham went to town for a little while, rushed through his business and came back to fish. He and Neyle got a nice dinner of fish. Had a *pencil* letter, short, from my considerate boy who thought we may not have heard of him often—so kind in him. Thank God, he continues well, although that is a trying climate. Last night I was *wretched* about it, and him, and was in an agony of tears for an hour. O God, spare my poor heart the misery which burdens so many hearts at this time! Did not sleep until daylight.

Went with Neyle and Mr. Higham to hear the band and see Dress Parade. Very pretty indeed. Sat in the Bath House talking Shakespeare. Mr. Higham told me, at my request, the story of Icarus from Ovid.

July 2, 1863. Mr. Higham gone back. Mama gone in to see Mary Screven who is ill. Poor Mrs. Burroughs![1] How *will* she survive the loss of her only daughter? God comfort her. Went rowing this afternoon, all of us and Baby, and then crabbing. A lovely evening but Camber did not like sitting so still, so had to bring him home.

1. Mrs. Joseph Burroughs, a friend who lived in Savannah.

Sat in the Bath house a long time having some *home-talks* with my husband. Oh! how much Parents have to make them anxious! Willie not yet come from town. Read the Richmond papers all the evening. Richmond probably threatened by Hooker,[2] Lee perhaps in possession of Harrisburg, Pennsylvania. Certainly has got immense stores by his advance—6,000 sheep and 5,000 head of cattle! The prisoners of the *Atlanta* reported at Hilton Head,[3] on their way to Fort Hudson (I think). How unjust to have surmised a *mutiny* of the crew![4] The New York *Herald* has the story, of course. Mary Screven still ill, Mamma reports.

July 3, 1863. Sent letters, several, and papers to Joseph Clay. He will not long be able, poor child, to hear so often. My heart sickens as the time draws near for Johnston's great battle! Oh! if we only had more men! Heard the children all their lessons. It is quick work, for they learn so rapidly, but, as they read so much, it is not worth while to keep them very long at their lessons.

Read aloud to Anna the scene between the two Talbots, father and son, on the Battle-field, the death of Warwick, etc., etc., etc.

July 4, 1863. Saturday. The *insolent Yankees* in our neighborhood are firing their guns in honor of *the day!* Little do *they* know or appreciate the precious *boon of Liberty* left us

2. Lee had failed to take the offensive after his victory over Burnside at Fredericksburg (Dec. 13, 1862). In the summer of 1863, outnumbered by the enemy, Lee continued on the defensive. He divided his army, sending Longstreet toward Suffolk. This gave General Joseph Hooker, who had replaced Burnside, a great advantage, he having about 130,000 troops to match against Lee's 60,000. With morale again high, Hooker sent Sedgwick to threaten Lee's right below Fredericksburg and took his own forces toward Chancellorsville. But the outcome of Chancellorsville (May 2-5) was another victory for the Confederates. Then Lee moved northward, which gave fear of another attempt by Hooker to move on Richmond. However, Hooker moved toward Washington to protect the Federal capital. Lee did plan to push Ewell as far as Harrisburg, but abandoned the plan. See Randall, *op. cit.*, 512-517.
3. The prisoners were quartered on the *Vermont*, which docked first at Hilton Head, then at Port Royal. *Official Records, Navy*, Ser. I, Vol. XIV, pp. 267-269.
4. Earlier rumors of a mutiny of the crew of the *Atlanta* were dispelled.

by our fathers on that glorious day, 1776! God grant that we Southerners, as a nation, may yet show the world an example of a refined and Christian nation who, having dearly bought this priceless boon, may know how to enjoy and value it! Went to see Mrs. Tucker[5] this evening. She is extremely kind to the soldiers around. If my family were not so large, and therefore continual calls on the servants' time, I would send them meals daily. As it *is*, I try to do a little good. For instance, while I have "fed" 18 or 20 white persons a day, at our house, I *know* she has had but two—herself and another. Adding four white servants, we "fed" one day, lately, twenty-three white persons and eight coloured! Octy Cohen[6] came to see us and stayed to tea. Nice boy. Neyle and Robert staid out so late we were all worried. I heard Freddie asking if "Uncle Neyle could swim"! I was full of foolish fancies and rejoiced to see them at nine o'clock! "Fish bit until so late that we were unwilling to come *at all*, except that you were uneasy"! Copied a great deal that has been absorbing me lately in Shakespeare.

July 5, 1863. Sunday. Not passed like Sunday. We all went to Church. A fancy seized me to take Cherry Cheeks and Dinah along, and when we got there we found Anna King[7] had brought *her* babe along. So they both came home together, in my carriage. Babe was charmed with the ride. Charles preached on the need of Chaplains to provide for the wonderful revival of religion in our army of Virginia and Tennessee. Oh Almighty God! Surely Thou art on our side! Such a thing is new in the annals of the world! Charles read many extracts showing the influence of the Holy Ghost on our Armies. My good, kind husband put in a large sum of

5. A neighbor on the southern point of White Bluff. Later William Neyle Habersham bought the Tucker place and added it to the Avon tract which it adjoined. Josephine named it Bonnie Doon because of her admiration for Robert Burns. When Robert Beverley, their son, married Margaret Cunningham Schley in 1872 Neyle and Josephine gave him the Tucker place. It is still in the possession of the family.
6. Son of Octavus Cohen, a commission merchant of Savannah.
7. Josephine's sister, wife of Charles King, the minister of the White Bluff Presbyterian Church.

money and gave me $20.00 for the purpose. Freddie gave $20.00, so our family did a *little*. Doctor Joseph Clay and Mary Anna came to dine, J. C. having business with Harrison's Regiment. So, with Charles and Anna and children, we had a large party. The two babes were very sweet and pretty together. I wish we could see more of my darling brother Joseph Clay. Mamma was quite in her *glory* with so many of her children! Willie came out this evening, bright and well. Says the Augusta girls and young men were charmed with their "Picnic" out here and with *this Lady!* and declared I was as young as a girl of eighteen! The vivacity of the young company is certainly infectious. They were pleased with Anna, as so perfectly ladylike, and, indeed, *everybody and everything*, including the dejeuner and hot, nice coffee! Had a sweet walk up and down the piazza, in the moonlight, with *mon bien aime*.

July 6, 1863. Good news from our Army, Lee in the rear of Washington between Hooker and *it*.[8] A delightful panic and horror taking possession of the Yankee mind,[9] which finds it very fine to stay at home in their comfortable farms and talk over the ravages, the fire and destruction visited upon our unoffending Southern plantations! God grant they may learn a lesson, under Lee, not pleasant to learn, and that will teach them how to come to their vile senses. Willie gone in, as he

8. On July 4, the day after his defeat at Gettysburg at the hands of General George G. Meade, Lee began an orderly retreat to Virginia. Randall thinks Meade lost a good opportunity to strike a crippling blow against Lee as he waited at Williamsport for the swollen Potomac to subside. Though Lee was "between Hooker and it [Washington]," his objective was to escape from the victorious Federals and protect his own capital city of Richmond. Lee crossed the Potomac on the night of the 13th. See Randall, *op. cit.*, 524.

9. Lee's retreat from Pennsylvania was not considered a defeat by Josephine. This same attitude was shared even by the men who fought with Lee at Gettysburg. Theodore F. Fogle wrote to his sister in Columbus, Georgia, that "we fell back at our leisure and offered him battle for five whole days but he would not attack us. Does that look like a defeat? Methinks not." This letter was written from camp near Bunker Hill (Berkeley Co.), Va., July 16, 1863. The letter is in the possession of Fogle's great-nephew, Dr. Thomas Harrold, Macon, Ga. Permission to use this item is gratefully acknowledged.

has a great deal of writing to do for Colonel Pelot[10] (he being his adjutant). Reading *Agatha's Husband*,[11] very good and extremely interesting. Mr. Higham quoted "thus shines a good deed in a naughty world." (*I* added the preceding line "How far the little candle throws its beams.") and asked me where it was. Something interrupted the talk, but afterwards I remembered it was in the serenity of domestic life and therefore must be in the garden scene at Portia's House. I looked for it and it was there, sure enough! It comes just after that lovely scene of refined and poetic home-life, where Jessica and the intellectual Lorenzo sit in the garden, hearing music coming "like the sweet sound, o'er a bank of violets, stealing and giving odor." Now I think of it, those lines come not there, but the Duke says them in *Twelfth Night*. I must tell Mr. Higham when I see him. We keep up a Shakespearian Battery!

July 7, 1863. Tuesday. Avon. Neyle sent in for the piano this morning, for which we were *all* anxious. *I* felt that l might thus divert my thoughts from dwelling too sadly on my child, my soldier boy. "I am never merry when I hear sweet music," says Jessica, but it soothes the soul and wins it from *gloom*. In the midst of our delight that the piano would be here

10. Lieutenant Commander Thomas P. Pelot was killed the next year leading a bold expedition which resulted in the capture of the United States Ship *Water Witch*. The *Water Witch*, Lieutentant Commander A. Pendergrast commanding, was one of the Federal ships blockading the Savannah port. In the dark of night Commander Pelot, with seven boats, 15 officers, and 117 men, floated down the Vernon River, drifting with the falling tide so as to avoid any noise of rowing and came upon the *Water Witch* as she lay anchored in Ossabaw Sound. They sprang on board without warning and a fight which lasted about half an hour ended with seven of Pelot's men killed, 12 wounded, and two Federals killed, 12 wounded. Though the Confederates and especially the Savannah people celebrated it as glorious achievement, actually the *Water Witch* was of no real service to the Confederacy. The Federals kept her bottled up in the harbor until Sherman reached Savannah (Dec. 21, 1864). She was then destroyed. See [William Harden], "The Capture of the U. S. Steamer 'Water Witch' in Ossabaw Sound, Ga., June 2-3, 1864," *Georgia Historical Quarterly*, III, 1 (March, 1919), 11-27.
11. A novel by Dinah Maria Mulock (Craik). It was published in London, 1853, in three volumes. She also wrote *Olive, The Ogilvies*, and other novels.

directly, we heard the sad news of sweet Mary Screven's[12] death—a fond Mother, devoted wife, and sweet friend! and a Christian, above all. So, Mamma, Neyle and I, *just* as the piano was at the door, went in to the funeral. "Shadow and shine is Life, flower and thorn." We returned, (Willie with us, who went with us to the Church) in the face of a heavy storm, but escaped it. We found the children enjoying the piano—the poor little Motherless ones of Mary Screven! God grant I may be of some service to my children and be impressed more and more by the awful responsibility resting upon a Mother of so many. My dear Husband caressed me, in mourning for the unhappiness of John Screven. And then that fine Major Giles[13] is dead and left a young widow. Oh! what is this world and the glory of it?

July 8, 1863. News sad enough, but not believed, that Vicksburg has fallen! It seems impossible after the repeated assurances that Pemberton's sustenance would last much longer. It would be dreadful, but it is not credited. Against this, we hear that Lee has fought with Meade (Hooker's Army) and beat and captured 40,000 prisoners![14] Pity they hadn't just *happened to chance* to get killed instead. We have all enjoyed the Piano. At first my fingers were really stiff, having played but once since poor Fred's death, poor fellow! But after practicing violently and difficult pieces for an hour or so, they are the same old fingers. Neyle says they do *finely*. Went this morning to Harrison Regimental Hospital,[15] taking Baby for the drive. Happy little boy, screaming out and beating Dinah with the fan! I found that a poor soldier had *just* died. They were laying him out and God knows my heart was full of

12. Wife of John Screven. She died at 36 years and three months.
13. Major John. R. Giles, 63rd Infantry Regiment, Georgia. See Charles Edgeworth Jones, *Georgia in the War, 1861-1865* (Augusta, Ga., 1909), 34.
14. Vicksburg surrendered July 4. 1863. Grant's report of the capture did not reach Lincoln until July 7, and on the next day, when General Banks captured Port Hudson, the news reached Savannah. By July 9 it was generally known that the Confederacy had been sliced in two. Confidence in Lee at Gettysburg continued, however, for some time after his retreat began on July 3.
15. On the Isle of Hope.

sympathy! Many a dear one is thus tended by stranger hands. Ah! Some have not even *that* attention! Oh! it is too pitiful for a Mother to think of! I sat alone a long time after I came home, trying to realize these things and to place my trust on a Merciful God! They were pleased to get the tureen of soup. I had One man changed from his bed in a hot corner to a nicer one where he could get the air. Tonight we played our dear old Kuhlau Sonatas.[16] Neyle's flute sounded sweetly. The children had, all of them, sung a long time. Mamie Cohen[17] also. Oh! how anxious! What a weight I feel about our boy! Dear child. How considerate he was to write so often—seven letters I think in three weeks, or less.

July 9, 1863. I am so anxious about our dear Boy that I felt really sick. Kept my bed all day but felt that I had better get up and *shake off*, if possible, a coming sickness. I have not had such a headache for years. We expected LeConte, Harden, Guerard, and Cohen[18] *to tea*, but they *did not* come, and missed the fine waffles, curd and cream and fine canteloupes. The girls dressed up and looked sweetly, but no beaux. I played for them to dance, Mamma fanning me all the time. I am thankful that we have the spirits for dancing and are not as many households are, shrouded in gloom. And to think that

16. Frederick Kuhlau was born in Ulzen, Hanover, Sept. 11, 1786, and died in Lyngbye, near Copenhagen, Mar. 12, 1832. He wrote many sonatas and sonatinas for piano, two and four hands, for instructive purposes primarily. He also wrote some operas which were well received at the time. See *Baker's Biographical Dictionary of Musicians*, 3rd ed., revised by Alfred Remy (New York, 1919), 493.
17. Daughter of Solomon Cohen, a prominent Savannah lawyer. He served as Postmaster at Savannah during the latter part of President Pierce's administration and the entire administration of President Buchanan. Mamie later married James Troup Dent.
18. Though Josephine refers to him as "Jerry" (see entry of July 10), she probably meant Julian LeConte, son of William and nephew of John LeConte, in whose home Joe Clay stayed when a student at South Carolina College. Harden could have been William D. Harden, a lieutenant on General Mercer's staff, William Harden, Co. F., 5th Georgia volunteer infantry, who later became librarian of the Georgia Historical Society, or John Harden, Jane LeConte Harden's son and cousin of Julian. John and Julian were both in the Chatham Artillery. See Joseph LeConte, *'Ware Sherman* (Berkeley, 1938), 82. Edgar Guerard has already been identified. Cohen was Octavus, Jr.

Vicksburg has fallen![19] Surely the press has been deceived all this time. "Gaunt famine" made surrender! and Johnston had not, up to the fourth, shot a gun! Per contra, Lee is victorious, the story of forty thousand prisoners true.[20] The crew of the *Atlanta* have returned to Savannah, being exchanged. They say dire necessity made them give up. The splinters dashed about in every direction! Freddie has grown more affectionate and demonstrative. We have enjoyed her visits much. Sent to the Hospital, as I was too unwell to go (as I do send every day). The sick man better. Only a few sick. My dear Husband so tender and concerned lest I should be sick! Finished *Agatha's Husband*. A good pleasant book, showing intimate acquaintance with woman's character, written by a woman and would please *only women*.

July 10, 1863. A lovely day. I feel better—still some headache. Freddie said goodbye to-day; left some pretty pieces of music to amuse me. Mamie Cohen, Neyle asked to stay longer. Robert expects to stay in tonight *if* they play one of Shakespeare's Tragedies at the Athenaeum.[21] I prefer their hearing *them*. Willie spending the day at Coffee Bluff[22] with Willie May.[23] Baby charmed with his $100. carriage—and Dinah also—just from Macon. Good Dinah! I'm glad she has this *help* in minding her Cherry Cheeks. The darling has such a sweet way, when his father kisses his *head*, of turning up his *little lips* to be kissed—a way of his own. The children crazy about bathing—terribly disappointed when they can't. Anna afraid of *nothing*, dives and swims, etc, etc. The child has a fund of energy in her composition *to do what she wants to do* that

19. After Sherman took Jackson, Mississippi, on May 14, he was able to keep Johnston east of the Big Black River and prevent his joining Pemberton at Vicksburg. Grant then began his assault on Vicksburg on May 18, and, with shells and grenades pouring into the city that ran so short of food that the people ate mule meat and fricasseed kitten, Vicksburg surrendered on Independence Day.
20. Josephine still thinks Lee has been victorious in Pennsylvania.
21. It had originally been called the Savannah Theater, and after the war reverted to its old name.
22. Where the Forest River runs into the Little Ogeechee.
23. Willie was one of their White Bluff neighbors. Ida was his sister. The White Bluff folks frequently fished at Coffee Bluff.

must be guided and watched. Par example, she wanted the Bath-house free of mud for Ellen Coleman[24] to bathe, and as the men were fishing or working in town, she tucked up her clothes, took a bucket and shovel, and did the whole business herself! And yet, often, *if she does not feel like it,* she frets over practicing.

Went to the Hospital. Found the three companies and regiments all gone, except the sick, to Pocataligo,[25] they say. Jerry LeConte did not get here after all. I wanted to show him attention for his Mother's sake. Carried a large tureen of soup for the sick soldiers, which they relished.

I ought to write letters to Essie, Ella,[26] and many others—the Fannys—but feel so anxious about Joseph Clay. The little girls delighted with *Edith's Ministry.*[27] Mary Belle could read until ten at night. As they want to return the book, I have let their lessons go for several days.

July 11, 1863. Oh! what sad news! the death of Langdon Cheves![28] A man noble, talented, in the prime of life and strength, who had entirely given himself up to his country's service, since the first gun was fired at Sumter had put aside all attention to his own interests, not even writing about such things and every moment of his time, all his talent, he gave to the engineering of these forts near Charleston! And killed before, perhaps, he could learn of the repulse of the enemy! This is the bitter drop in a soldier's death, to die supposing

24. Neyle's sister, Ellen Habersham (Mrs. William Coleman).
25. One now goes through Pocataligo from Savannah to Charleston over the Coastal Highway, U. S. 17. It is 29 miles from the Savannah River on the South Carolina side.
26. "Essie" was Esther Habersham, daughter of Richard Habersham. Ella was the daughter of Captain Thomas Newell. Ella married Leonard Y. Gibbes.
27. A novel by Harriet B. McKeever, published in Philadelphia, ca. 1860.
28. Captain Langdon Cheves (1814-1863) was killed at Morris Island the day before. (Brig.-Gen. Roswell S. Ripley's report, July 22, 1863, *Official Records, War,* Ser. I, Vol. XXVIII, pt. 1, pp, 370-374.) His father, Judge Langdon Cheves, had been mentioned as a worthy successor to Calhoun in the Senate in 1850. He had opposed secession of South Carolina in an independent action in 1850 and had favored co-operation with other slave-holding states. See Wallace, *op. cit.,* III, 126-127; South Carolina Archives Department, Columbia, S. C.

all was lost. Poor Sydney Johnston was dead before the hour of victory.[29] *Ill news is rife.* Vicksburg fallen! Charleston again attacked by land and water, repulsed they say, the enemy was, by both. Lee fallen back from so near Washington because of want of transportation. The only really *good* news is New Orleans again in our hands, recaptured by General Taylor.[30] Some peace, perhaps, for the poor ill-treated citizens. Of course we long to hear where our boy is! Two *very long* letters and one short note in pencil (on dress parade) came today. Thank God for them and for all his goodness in allowing me to hear so much of my child and always that he *is well*—now nursing a friend—sitting up at night. Just from a long march to Edward's Depot. He always writes in good spirits but confesses himself homesick, having had but three letters, one of perhaps fifteen or eighteen. *I* got all of *his*. Oh! We are anxious to hear how Charleston is faring! All the women and children, and men over seventy years ordered out of the City. Went to see Mrs. Harrison. Had a telegram from Colonel Harrison[31] saying his regiment[32] was badly cut up. Did not mention the loss. Cherry Cheeks has such a sweet winning way of calling any one by doubling the fingers of his fat, dimpled little hand! Grandma made a pair of pretty shoes in her neat way for him, but he has to go barefoot 'till cold weather. He *won't* have them near him.

No music tonight, all too dull. Mamma tired from her trip to town, and all off to bed early.

29. General Albert Sidney Johnston was killed in the first day's fighting in the Battle of Shiloh, April 6-7, 1862. In his moment of victory he was hit in the leg, and with an artery severed, he bled to death. Jefferson Davis mourned his death as an "irreparable loss." Beauregard took command on the seventh, but Grant forced him back to Corinth.
30. Lieutenant General Richard Taylor of Louisiana, son of Zachary Taylor. It was he who surrendered what remained of the Confederate forces east of the Mississippi to General E. R. S. Canby at Citronelle, near Mobile, Alabama, on May 4, 1865.
31. Col. George Paul Harrison, Jr.
32. The Thirty-Second Georgia, sent to the relief of the garrison on James Island. See Ripley's report, July 22, 1863, in *Official Records, War*, Ser. I, Vol. XXVIII, pt. 1, pp. 370-374.

July 12, 1863. Sunday. Mr. Kollock[33] dined. I'm sure he seems a good kind man, but oh! how hard to talk to! *Neyle* had him though! We all went to Church but dear Mamma, who is not well. Charles King looked very doleful and depressed about the news, although he *does* preach *faith and trust.* He is the bluest looking person I've seen. I don't believe they will do much harm to Charleston, but I fear many lives will be lost in her defence. Neyle says Gnospelius,[34] the pianist, spoke to him from the resemblance to *me*, in the eyes, he said, and Joseph Clay told me he recognized *him* in Mobile for his likeness to *me.* J. C. is always told he resembles me. Willy not so often, and although I think there is a family resemblance between the two brothers, I wonder they should be taken for each other which they *have been*. Robert is much like Joseph Clay and so is dear Camber.

Robert Beverley and I sang hymns after the little girls had done their singing and gone to bed.

July 13, 1863. Monday. Attack on Charleston continued. Enemy repulsed, except that they have gained a footing on the lower part of Morris Island. Much anxiety felt *since* they have a foothold there. Things seem better than we heard with Lee. Fighting at Jackson. Oh! is our child there? Heavenly Father, compassionate us! and spare him!

Tried to practise a little to keep my spirits up, and read Fantine, Victor Hugo's last book.[35] Have read nearly two thirds and see nothing that shows genius except in about six pages. *Trop prononce*, as those French books usually are! *Je ne les aime pas.*

Neyle wrote a long letter to Joseph Clay. Went to the two Hospitals. Saw one poor man, very low I thought, his eyes glazed and hands cold. My attention was attracted by

33. Dr. Phineas Miller Kollock, a well-known Savannah physician and vestryman of Christ Church. The Kollock place was next to the Habersham property on the White Bluff road.
34. G. A. Gnospelius, organist of Christ Church, choir master and music teacher.
35. *Les Miserables* (1862), Hugo's great social novel. In order to support herself and infant, Fantine sells her body, but redeems herself through maternal love.

seeing him fall back as they tried to give him soup which I carried. The idea! the poor man was all but dying—perfectly unconscious, and these two stewards or nurses trying to make him eat the soup. They soon found out from what I said that he was all but dying and began to show some interest. But there was no one brushing the flies and attending to him when I went there.

Felt very little like it, but played the piano for a dozen soldiers who seated themselves on the green, evidently to hear music! The little girls said their lessons well. Anna practised nicely, but *no lessons* is the order of the day since Mamie Cohen is here.

July 14, 1863. Tuesday. Nothing new from Charleston. Mrs. Dillon[36] gone to nurse the sick of the Guards. Went in to see dear Sister Mary. She looks pretty well, always serene and peaceful. Oh! how wonderful is the *Grace* of God to support the bruised spirit! Poor Aunt Susan[37] tries to exert *herself*, looks better. Dear father looks so well and healthy. Willie went yesterday to Isle of Hope to see Mary Anna. Brother Joseph Clay gone to Charleston. Found precious Cherry Cheeks had been calling Mamma all day. He was really enchanted to see me. Neyle had caught plenty of fish.

July 15, 1863. Wednesday. Robert rode out early this morning bringing Frank Neufville,[38] brought sad news. Even *I* began to feel there is much cause for gloom. Lee has fallen back to the Potomac *instead* of advancing to Washington as we hoped. Bragg had to make a move, which leaves Georgia more open.[39] Already we see "*plans* of raids" into Georgia.

36. Wife of John R. Dillon, Secretary of the Hibernian Society. They had a son, John, Jr., in service.
37. Susan Dorothy Habersham, third daughter of Major John Habersham. She married Joseph Habersham, Jr., her first cousin.
38. Edward Frank Neufville, son of the Reverend Edward Neufville. His father was Rector of Christ Church, Savannah (1827-1850), and his mother was Mary Fenwick Kollock Neufville. Frank was a 2nd. Lt. in the Marine Corps stationed at Savannah.
39. Rosecrans had moved his army out of Murfreesboro in June, having defeated Bragg there six months before (Battle of Murfreesboro or Stone's River, Dec. 31-Jan. 3, 1862-63). He then maneuvered Bragg out of Chattanooga. Confederate strategists have been very critical of Bragg's evacuation of Chattanooga. See Randall, *op. cit.*, 528, 533.

We shall have trouble, they say, with the Yankees who have got a foothold on Morris Island,[40] and above all!—without a hint of such a thing—Port Hudson[41] has fallen leaving us without two of the most important posts on the Mississippi River! Well! that is a sentence full enough of disaster! Again *we hear* we have beat the enemy at *Jackson*.[42] In a fight on the field we are always successful. Oh! was our child there, and how did he fare? I cannot write on this subject! Let me thank God that there is left me a compassionate Jesus to whom I may pour out my *fears* and ask for help.

Went to the Hospitals—found one man still very low. How great a lesson is this! to lie utterly *unconscious* for days, seemingly no pain and certainly no mental trouble. How about the poor creature's Soul? This is no time for *that soul* to bethink itself of the claims of eternity! Like Victor Hugo's book less and less. My dear Shakespeare is my comfort. Fighting at Jackson—the Sharpshooters engaged—*which must* be Walker's Division,[43] in which our child is. Robert stayed out with Frank Neufville. Little girls said their lessons well; Lilla is surprisingly intelligent in Grammar. Willie stayed in town to see one of Shakespeare's plays acted. No further news from Charleston.

July 16, 1863. Friday.[44] Rain all day—a doleful time, so anxious. Did some sewing. No farther news of interest. Oh! could I but hear from our darling! God bless him and keep him safe. Wrote to Essie to divert my mind. Heard from Dr. Joseph Clay at Charleston, quite well.

July 17, 1863. I cried myself to sleep last night—aye—and many another night! Thankful for the sweet rest I had.

40. In Charleston harbor.
41. One hundred miles down the Mississippi River from Vicksburg. General Nathaniel P. Banks captured Port Hudson on July 8, 1863, just four days after the surrender of Vicksburg.
42. On the 12th a Federal assault was repulsed, but on the night of the 16th Johnston withdrew his army toward Meridian where he established his headquarters. See Evans, *op. cit.,* VII, Miss., 162.
43. The Second Georgia Battalion ("Sharpshooters") was in Walker's division.
44. Thursday. She was confused as to the day of the week.

After being awake *half* of the night before that I feel dull and heavy—listless. Will copy some beautiful hymns for occupation—copied *often* before—Matthew 6. 10—

> My God, my father, while I stray,
> Far from my home, on Life's rough way,
> Oh! teach me from my heart to say,
> "Thy will be done."
>
> If Thou shouldst call me to resign
> What most I prize - it ne'er was mine,
> I only yield Thee what was Thine,
> "Thy will be done."
>
> E'en if again I ne'er should see
> The friend more dear than life to me,
> E'er long we both shall be with Thee;
> "Thy will be done."
>
> Should pining sickness waste away
> My life in premature decay,
> My father, still I strive to say,
> "Thy will be done."
>
> If but my fainting heart be blest
> With Thy sweet spirit for its guest,
> My God, to Thee I leave the rest.
> "Thy will be done."
>
> Renew my will from day to day,
> Blend it with Thine, and take away
> All that now makes it hard to say
> "Thy will be done."[45]
>
> Then, when on Earth I breathe no more,
> The prayer, oft mix'd with tears before;
> I'll sing upon a happier shore,
> "Thy will be done."

45. Charlotte Elliott. This hymn was reprinted in the *Free Church Hymn-Book* from Miss Elliott's *Hours of Sorrow Cheered and Comforted* (5th ed., 1856). Charlotte Elliott was born at Westfield Lodge, Brighton, England, Mar. 18, 1789. She became a permanent invalid in 1821. Her familiar hymn, "Just As I Am," was published in the *Invalid's Hymn-Book* in 1836. Miss Elliott contributed 115 pieces to that volume.

Certainly to say this with entire submission and trust is the height of human happiness! There are innocent pleasures and enjoyments surely, for God has not blessed us in vain with sweet affections; pure tastes, but how frail their tenure! "Sunshine and shade is Life, flower and Thorn!"[46]

Little girls said lessons nicely. Mamie Cohen went this morning. A nice, good child, well brought up. I hope now Anna will give *me* some of her time and read, etc., with me. I need never ask the other little girls to read, they are always at it.

Young Dr. Bonner came to tea, a simple, plain South Carolina up country man—knows Dr. Stephen Habersham[47] of Richland Hospital. Has lost eleven cousins, a father and *two brothers* in this war. I played a long time for him. He is going to bring a man that plays the Banjo well to serenade Anna. Ella Newell spent the day.

No farther news from Charleston. We fear the enemy are strengthening themselves. How sad the other day the burial of two young men, nineteen years old, of the Savannah Guards, on one bier in Savannah. Fighting at Jackson—on fifteenth.

July 18, 1863. Sunday. Dugas[48] came out to stay a day or two with Willy. Robert brought papers—*Jackson evacuated* after so many days of fighting—of which we have *no particulars*. News will be hard to get at now, as that is the mail route. Oh! I trust my child has been receiving my letters! More lately. How homesick it must have made him! And I'm sure our messages of love, from all of us, would have been valued by him all this time that he writes *us* so frequently, and yet *he* cannot hear.

46. "But the first that ever I bare was
      dead before he was born,
      Shadow and shine is life, little Annie,
      flower and thorn."
  Tennyson, "The Grandmother," v. 15. This is the second time that Josephine has quoted this passage, and this time she changes the word order.
47. Neyle's first cousin.
48. A friend of Willie's, probably from Augusta.

Nothing new from Charleston except that we went to surprise the enemy (Chatham Artillery among them) and found negroes there. Many were killed, some captured. As a body they *ran*. Every confidence is felt in Beauregard,[49] but Ripley[50] is talked against, a drunkard, it seems, and a Yankee! The Guards, having been much exposed, are now placed in Charleston.

Emma McAllister very ill, poor creature! Busy sewing today, with some practising. Lilla surprises me more and more by her talent for music, but is very impatient of correction. Dear Cherry Cheeks loves me more and more every day. Calls beautifully with his hand. Ella Newell says he is perfectly beautiful—such a splendid complexion. So sorry dear Ellen did not make us a visit nor come to spend today. Goes soon to Clarksville.[51] Robert and Neyle very busy over Robert's mast and sail. Copied Shakespeare to amuse my mind. Dreamed last night that I had, and was looking over, a great quantity of my beloved Joseph Clay's hair. Oh God! keep me from distressing thoughts.

The wife of the man ill at Harrison's Hospital has come; looks, as they always do, unconcerned.

July 19, 1863. Sunday. Felt very dull and heavy, and did not go to Church. Helped to mind Cherry Cheeks. The little girls disappointed because Daisy[52] did not come with her father.

49. Pierre Gustave Toutant Beauregard. This dapper little "Napoleon in Gray" made a hit with the Charleston and Savannah ladies. It was he who captured the Federal Fort Sumter to begin the war. He was back again in Charleston in 1863 charged with defending the South Carolina and Georgia coasts. The success of his efforts is attested by the fact that, though the Federals repeatedly assaulted the batteries by land and sea, Charleston remained in Confederate possession until the end of the war.
50. Brigadier-General Roswell Sabine Ripley, a native of Ohio, was at odds with Beauregard at this time. See J. G. de Roulhac Hamilton's sketch of Ripley in *Dictionary of American Biography*, XV, 625-626.
51. A popular summer resort in the mountains in Habersham County. The county was named in honor of Col. Joseph Habersham, who had a summer home there. The county was laid out in 1818.
52. Daughter of Charles and Anna King, called "Daisy," but her name was Mary Josephine. She married Reuben G. Clark.

Five gun-boats, or some kind of vessel, off Beuly.[53] Lieutenant Hunter,[54] who dined with Willie, yesterday, says the Battery is a good one. The last gun a very fine one. Feel very dull and weary. Not one word of our child when we *know* that there has been fighting about Jackson since the eleventh, perhaps before. Dreamt of him last night. Wrote to my dear Joseph Clay.

July 20, 1863. Monday. Made myself busy sewing for Willie all day. He and Dugas gone to Augusta. Heard the little girls' lessons, and Mary Belle read and got me to explain parts of *Macbeth* and the death of Clarence.[55] Was occupied an hour and three quarters with Shakespeare! No fears for *her*. She will always find her own equal to her amusement and entertainment. Little girls went over to the Salt Works with Anna, where they were met by Mary Wylly.[56] Anna rejoiced to stay there a few days. The girls (Newells)[57] had a fine story to tell of their going sailing with some of those Crackers, soldiers, who know nothing of boats. A storm came up, black as pitch, wind died out, and they did not get home till four o'clock Sunday night, or *morning*. Aunt Hetty[58] must have had a pleasant time, fancying them captured by the Yankee Blockaders—several of which are *not* distant. Nothing new from Jackson, and no news from my dear boy. Oh! may I try with all my heart to be cheerful and not give up to anxiety.

Little girls went fishing with their father. I staid at home with Cherry Cheeks. Some soldiers admired him on the green in his carriage. The child nearly jumps out with delight when *I* drag him. Dear brother Joseph Clay sent us his watch and

---

53. Beaulieu, on the Vernon River, three miles from White Bluff. There was a Confederate battery there.
54. Lt. Charles C. Hunter, Willie's friend.
55. *Richard the Third*, I. 4. 274.
56. Mary Wylly Newell. She later married Lewis T. Turner.
57. Ella, Mary, Nannette, and Roberta. Captain Newell had moved his family to Georgia from Connecticut. Nannette later married James B. West. Roberta never married—or, as the darkies said, she didn't "signify."
58. Hester R. Adams, second wife of Captain Thomas Newell.

breastpin to keep—sent Neyle from Charleston. May God protect this darling beloved brother! He is very dear to me, has *always been* my special pet.

Cheering news from Charleston. Enemy repulsed at Fort Wagner,[59] having bombarded it for eleven hours and made an infantry attack *besides*. Our Georgians and the Carolinians show great bravery and determination. Things look brighter there. If bravery and patriotism can avail, Charleston will never fall into the hands of these dastardly hordes, with their *negro* regiments. Dr. Bonner (of First artillery) brought the Banjo player as he promised Anna. He played as well as one *can* play the Banjo, I suppose, and had an excellent voice—sang untiringly and would have sung an hour longer if Dr. Bonner had not made the move. Slept well last night and am thankful for it. Mamma expected this evening. Mr. Higham must be in hot water now.

July 25, 1863. Saturday. Neyle's birthday. I have felt so wearied with anxiety that I have not written since Monday. Thank God! Oh! thank God! we have heard from our boy—in the midst of the shelling Grant keeps up, to be sure, but was well on the fifteenth. "In line of Battle, *near* Jackson." Jackson has been since burnt, the Depot and Rail Road stock destroyed. Grant victorious—although in all the little *skirmishes* (in several of them Joseph Clay was) the enemy was repulsed. Lee still inactive and all the results which we *now* see of his invasion is the longest of long sad, mournful lists of "Killed and wounded at Gettysburg" *which fill* our papers.[60]

Charleston quiet—the enemy repulsed *bravely* and totally on Saturday after shelling Fort Wagner for eleven hours and leading large bodies of white and black infantry up to the very parapets. Dr. Joseph Clay returned—well. Thank God for that, for the peril was great at Morris Island. So anxious to

59. Vigorous attacks were made upon the city in July and August from land and sea, but Beauregard's men withstood all assaults, and, though Sumter was reduced to ashes, the Confederates continued to hold it until February, 1865, when it was abandoned to the victorious Union troops. Randall, *op. cit.*, 591.
60. Now she knows what really happened at Gettysburg on July 3.

see him. Mama came back from Isle of Hope, not at all well. Anna has been spending a week with Mary Wylly and has just returned, her white skin which we were all admiring so much last week terribly burnt and *brown.* Had fine time, and saw Captain Twiggs[61] whom Dr. J. C. brought from Morris Island, wounded by a shell—has no command hardly over his limbs.

The little girls have said prettily their lessons this week, *although* Daisy is with them. They do very nicely in French. Since I have felt better about my dear child, I have been singing with the children and R. B. every night. Robert will sing admirably. He enjoys singing with me which is a great inducement for me to teach him my songs. Mary Belle has been reading such passages of Shakespeare this week as I select, of course—incidents, plots, tales, etc., to amuse her. One day she kept reading in Shakespeare for nearly two hours, so much that I excused her her lessons. Sorry Mary Owens[62] would not come to stay with me a little while. Wrote Mde. Guyol[63] yesterday, and Fannie Manigault and Willie (at Augusta with Dugas). Much rain this week—splendid thunder storms. I have sewed a good deal, and read a great deal in Shakespeare—*Lear, Macbeth, Henry VIII* and *Taming of the Shrew.* So few men sick at the Hospitals, do not now go often. Mr. Higham writes he is coming for two days. I don't think Neyle enjoys his company very much *out here, he is so restless.* He is delightful company for *now and then,* but not for a constancy.

The papers are picking at Pemberton for giving up Vicksburg. He may not be to blame, but *anyhow,* we have suffered with the two Yankees who manage our affairs. Lovell[64.] in

---

61. Captain H. D. W. Twiggs, severely wounded in Federal assault on Fort Wagner, July 18, 1863.
62. Daughter of George Owens. She never married.
63. Mathilde Guyol of New Orleans, a friend.
64. Major-General Mansfield Lovell, born in Washington, lost New Orleans to Farragut, Apr. 23, 1862, more through "governmental ineptitude" than his own inability. See *Dictionary of American Biography,* XI, 442.

New Orleans and Pemberton[65] in Vicksburg, and as to Ripley in Charleston, it is well we have Beauregard *there*, as he[66] is a drunken thing.

God bless my precious husband and keep him at my side as long as *I* live is my prayer. His forty-sixth birthday. We grow older, but age can bring only increase of affection. We have joyed and sorrowed together for twenty-three years. Truly may I say my husband's love has gladdened my happy hours and lessened and soothed my sad ones.

July 26, 1863. Sunday. All went to Church today, I feeling much better since hearing from Joseph Clay, and what was our delight to have Charles King hand us *two* letters from him—one so late as nineteenth. He tells of great *suffering* and disorder in the retreat from Jackson—marching until three o'clock at night through rain, mud, and wearied with thirst. Out of the Eighth Georgia men, only forty marched into camp near Brandon.[67] Out of two thousand [in] Gist's Brigade, only six hundred marched into Camp. Many went in sick and dying. Some gave out a *hundred yards* only from the resting place. Poor fellows! Thank God, he passed through all the shelling at Jackson unhurt except for a minnie ball which *glanced* over his right ear, leaving a lump. I remember he was playing with his very sharp sword[68] one day out here last year—about one year ago—and cut his *left* ear so badly that Mamma had to court plaster and bandage it up. I'm so happy that he has been so fortunate as, at last, to get thirteen letters by one mail—seven of them from me.

65. Gen. John C. Pemberton was also a Northern man, born in Philadelphia.
66. Meaning Ripley. Thus she names three "Northerners" who fought for the Southern cause, but she has little regard for any of them. Yet, for such men loyally serving the Confederacy—despite Josephine's attitude toward them—there were Southern Unionists, like Generals Canby, Buell, and "Rock of Chickamauga" Thomas, and Admiral Farragut, to counterbalance them.
67. Brandon, Mississippi, 13 miles east of Jackson.
68. His sword is now in the possession of William Etsel Snowden, III, Atlanta, Robert's great-grandson.

The little girls and Edward and Dah⁶⁹ have gone to walk on the Bluff this *splendid* afternoon. Such a glorious sea breeze, and the high tide looking beautifully. Dear Cherry Cheeks amazed us all by showing the greatest delight when Neyle gave him the reins, on coming from Church, to ride about the yard. He held them *tight* and wouldn't give them up.

Nothing new from Charleston; fearful lists of "killed and wounded" still in the papers from Gettysburg—Lee's battle. Twelve officers from Isle of Hope at Church. Terrell Artillery still here.

July 27, 1863. Monday. Read, sewed, heard the children their lessons, practised a couple of hours. My dear husband came out in the evening in a hard rain, feeling feverish—took medicine. He made me and the children play and sing after tea, felt better. Dr. Joseph Clay spent the day. So glad to see him. He had a trying time at Morris Island, his feeling heart sympathizing so deeply with the suffering. One Colonel Simpkins [*sic*], of South Carolina⁷⁰ was brought to him, dying. Dr. J. C. told him he had but a very little while to live. He was much shocked, but said solemnly, "I have a most interesting family"—then stopped and said, "Tell my wife I died for my God and my Country." Many other things he told us made the tears roll down our cheeks. Langdon Cheeves was the *first* man killed—in a wide open space, and he the only man in it! Crossing the enclosure to reach the parapet.

July 28, 1863. Tuesday. My dear husband feels badly, but has no fever, thank God. I have been having the bushes etc. trimmed. The grass and verdure are lovely. The whole house was alarmed this morning by poor little Mary Belle falling on her eye and cheek. He escaped.⁷¹ She held him tight. She and Lilla could hardly be pacified, and when Anna ran off

---

69. Dinah, Negro nurse who nursed not only Josephine's children but, later, Anna's also.
70. Lt.-Col. J. C. Simkins fell on July 18 in the second assault on Battery Wagner. He was "standing on the ramparts and cheering his artillery when he fell." Evans, *op. cit.*, V (S. C.), 240.
71. Edward Camber, the baby.

with Baby, thinking he was hurt, Mary Belle and Lilla *actually* thought he was nearly killed. Lilla was found on her knees thanking God he had escaped. I, happily, was fast asleep. There never was a greater fright in hall or kitchen! Wrote my boy.

Reading Lord Eldon's life[72] (Lord Chancellor). Read *In Memoriam* yesterday. These words struck me as applicable to Lord Bacon, "Let then silence guard his fame."

July 29, 1863. Wednesday. Read the life of Sir Thomas More,[73] Chancellor. How interesting! What a guileless simplicity of character conbined with deep wisdom! And to think that such a man was condemned to death because he would not violate his conscience! His domestic life is really touchingly beautiful.

Our figs are nice. Neyle is very careful I shall get the best and the lion's share too. Practised and sang, my voice coming back somewhat. Cough better. Received four letters from dear Joseph Clay—two notes, and one of them a very long and interesting letter. A young girl had pinned a feather in his hat saying she hoped if he was struck it "would be as lightly as a feather," and the next day, about the same hour, the ball (minnie) glanced the feather and just grazed his ear and made a lump. It was curious. Children said their French lessons, prettily.

July 30, 1863. Thursday. Read, practised, heard lessons and sewed. While sewing I let my thoughts dwell on my son, breathing prayers for his safety and welfare, temporal and eternal. Wrote dear Joseph Clay.

72. Horace Twiss, *Life of Lord Chancellor Eldon* (London and Philadelphia, 1844, 2 vols.).
73. This may have been one of several editions of the biography by his son-in-law, William Roper, first published in 1626 under the title, *The Life, Arraignment, and Death of that Mirrour of all Honour and Virtue, Sir Thomas More.* But John O'Hagen says, "By far the fullest and most interesting biography is that published some eighty years after his death by his great grandson and namesake, Thomas More." John O'Hagen, "Introduction" to More's *Utopia*, Everyman's edition (London, 1946), vii.

Charleston quiet. Heard from Mde. Guyol, a pretty letter in French. Johnson's [sic] army resting. Grant's gone to Vicksburg. Lee quiet. Morgan the Raider captured[74] after doing immense injury to the Yankees. Last night the Banjo sounded again in our piazza for Anna's benefit. Dr. Bonner bringing the trumpeter. He has a good voice, but what a worthless instrument is the Banjo! Felt very unwell for two days past. Read Shakespeare and Lord Eldon's life.

July 31, 1863. Friday. My dear Mother's birthday—a lovely cool day. I wish Anna King could have come out. We enjoyed some cake and *wine* she made for dear Mamma! I wonder if any of her daughters will be active and smart at sixty-eight years as Mamma is! She has wonderful energy.

All admired the splendid moonlight which fell upon the water in long streams, which looked like the glorious casements described in *Arabian Nights* where brilliant lights shine through—way down in the depths of the sea in the Mermaid's halls. Little children dancing after tea. Had music and singing. Robert in town to attend the Theatre. Wrote Willy.

74. Like Mosby's Rangers in Virginia, General John H. Morgan's raiders operated in Kentucky. Both men harassed the Union troops and kept many companies "fruitlessly occupied" in petty warfare away from the major battle fields. See Ella Lonn, *Desertion During the Civil War* (New York, 1928), 119. Morgan was captured on the Ohio River on July 26. See Evans, *op. cit.*, IX, 173. For Brig.-Gen. B. W. Duke's account of the Ohio raid, including map, see *Battles and Leaders of the Civil War*, 4 vols. (New York, 1956. New edition), III, 634-635.

"Not in anger smite us, Lord!
Spare thy people, spare!
If Thou mete us due reward,
We must all despair."
—Albinus, hymn

FIRE IN THE ASHES

The Federal gun boats blasted away at Fort Sumter and the Charleston batteries in August, reducing Sumter to ashes, but there was no surrender. The fire of the Yankees was matched by the spirit of the defenders of Charleston. Defiance continues strong in Josephine's heart as she reads the dispatches down on the Vernon River below Savannah, but the discipline of war brings her to her knees in humility and contrition.

August 1, 1863. Saturday. July has been a gloomy month for our beloved Confederacy! Beginning with every cheerful aspect, everybody confident, yet early in July Vicksburg surrendered. Lee's invasion was unfortunate; he had to recross the Potomac. Fort Hudson surrendered, Jackson evacuated and burnt, and all the country round about devastated. *Morgan the Raider* captured with many men. Bragg had to retreat from the fertile country of East Tennessee and fall upon Chattanooga without fighting and overcoming Rosencranz.[1] Charleston invested! To be sure, *so far*, we have repulsed the enemy there, but *can* Fort Wagner stand much more? All this is a heavy gloomy list. Reports, too, of coming raids in Alabama and Northern Georgia. So much for July. Yet we are *not* despondent. Reverses will but nerve to greater energy and self sacrifice the Southern arm and the Southern heart.

1. General William Starke Rosecrans, a native of Ohio. Josephine's spelling is close to the mid-seventeenth century form when the Rosenkrans family came to America. Then, too, Josephine may be reflecting the influence of Shakespeare, of whom she was so fond. The name is spelled "Rosencrantz" in *Hamlet*. Early in July Rosecrans had maneuvered Bragg out of Shelbyville and Tullahoma, Tennessee, back into Chattanooga.

A nice long letter from Joseph Clay—Army at rest. He begs Anna to make him some nic-nacs. Dr. Joseph Clay went to Morris Island this morning.[2] God preserve his precious, valuable life!

August 2, 1863. Sunday. A rain nearly all the morning, but my good husband *rarely* stays from Church. All went but Anna and I and precious Cherry Cheeks. Little Daisy went home from Church with her father, the little girls sorry to give her up. Sweet little thing. The nights are splendid, the river lovely by moonlight. Mary Belle said, as it shone upon her at tea table through the window, "Oh, thou Moon! thou *look* as if thou wert calling me to Heaven." She reads so much poetry she frequently uses Thou in speaking.

August 3, 1863. Monday. Nothing new from Charleston, but that Fort Wagner is firing into the enemy's batteries. A letter from our dear boy, one from Willie. Delighted more than ever with Miss Clara and others. Children said their lessons *beautifully*. While Daisy was here it was only a farce, learning lessons—too full of play.

August 4, 1863. So delightful to have my voice again in some degree, not as full as of yore. I sing constantly. Always *did* love to sing with my children, and Robert will sing well. Mary Belle, I think, will have a very fine voice. She has a great idea of singing. We sing at night, all of us. Have been reading Shakespeare and *Le Philosophe Sous les Toits*,[3] sweet little book. Took a delightful walk with Mamma and the children, and met Dr. Bonner, who joined us, all the way. Was glad he said *no* to an invite to tea as it is stupid for Neyle.

Neyle and Robert came out with a *report* that the enemy had landed in force at Montgomery[4] and would march and

---

2. Josephine's doctor brother went often to Charleston to attend the wounded.
3. Emil Souvestre, *Le Philosophe Sous les Toits* (Paris, 1850). This popular work, published by Michel Levy frères, was recognized by the French Academy in 1851 and was reprinted many times between 1850 and 1863. It is a Breton story.
4. Montgomery is on the Vernon River, just below Avon.

seize Savannah! So much did we bother ourselves about it, that all went crabbing. Neyle and Robert went to Coffee Bluff for the afternoon taking, by the way, a bateau which had to be *lifted from the water here,* put in a cart, taken to Coffee Bluff, there lifted into the water again. They fished a couple of hours, bateau lifted back into cart, brought home, and there it stands in the lawn, till it can be put back into the water! *Verily,* that husband of mine *loves to fish!*[5] Truly glad am I he has this sport to refresh him after his town-work.[6]

Sorry the draft[7] took place today and Willie, an adjutant, *not here*—in Augusta. Nice letters to Lilla and Anna from J. C. who begs *Anna* to make so and so for him! I think Mary and I will have to lend a big part of the helping! Took a sweet walk with Camber in his carriage—far on the Bluff. Sang plenty of songs and some nice new, *no, old* French songs, that were sent away a long time.

August 5, 1863. Anna gone to town today to see the folks. Baby's voice sounded loud in laughter. Dear Sister Mary! The time approaches which marks the anniversary of her son's death.[8] Poor thing! What a visitation was *that* of the Almighty's hand! *Who,* humanly speaking, less deserved a

5. One of the pictures in the back hall at Avon is a painting of a large salmon, by W. M. Brackett, Neyle's friend, a devotee of salmon fishing.
6. This rice merchant was so prominent a fisherman that he had a fly named for him.
7. By the Act of April 16, 1862, the Confederacy drafted for military service all white men from 18 to 35 years of age for three years. By February 17, 1864, the age group was extended to include men from 17 to 50.
8. Lt. Robert Habersham Elliott. "Dear Sister Mary," Robert's mother, was Neyle's half-sister. She had married William Elliott, brother of Bishop Elliott. She was known as "St. Mary" because of her deep spirituality and her many kind deeds. Robert married another Mary Elliott. Robert died as so many other Confederate soldiers did, not of wounds but of camp fever which developed into pneumonia. His death occurred on Aug. 13, 1862. He was a 1st Lt., Co. D., Chatham County (Olmstead's) 1st Regt. Ga. Infantry. Confederate Pension and Record Dept. He left his young wife a four-months-old son, Arthur Beverley. Arthur grew up and married Mary White, daughter of the Rev. Robb White, Rector of Christ Church. After Robert's death Mary married again, this time Joseph Alston Huger, a rice planter of the well-known South Carolina family.

needed chastisement? I think often of Mary Elliott[9] and Leila![10] Figs are plenty and nice. Neyle watches me like a cat to see that I enjoy them. I miss Anna reading *Great Expectations*[11] today aloud.

August 6, 1863. Thursday. Anna returned last evening full of *talk*. She found it awfully hot in town, thermometer 90° out here. The strong sea breeze blew all day, and it was a delightful day. She says Georgia Gilliam[12] is dead, poor thing! She is at rest! She mourned the loss of her husband, and was in most wretched health! She says nearly all the girls of her age are going, or have gone, to boarding school. I hope to have her taught *at home*. William Habersham[13] came out with Neyle. Practised well, heard the children all their lessons. Lilla says her French wonderfully and is more fond of it than Anna. Mary Belle does extremely well, her memory aids her. Cherry Cheeks has learnt a new style of playing—with the *thumb* alone, the other fingers of his wee tiny fat hand up in the air. Tries to say "Give me"—understands many things. So busy sewing while sitting with Mamma, I did not read much. Was glad to be able to tell Robert all the story of *King Lear* and *Romeo and Juliet*. He seems interested in Shakespeare. Lilla and I played duets very nicely, that is, I played bass to her treble—four hands. William Habersham was delighted. Took a long delightful walk, Mamma and the little girls and Babe.

August 7, 1863. Friday. Lilla wrote such a remarkably correct and pretty letter to Joseph Clay that I sent it to Charles King to see. A long, pretty letter, not a word spelt wrong, and all the punctuation perfectly correct. I told Charles that some of it was owing to the care with which

9. Robert's widow.
10. Mary Elliott's sister. She married Frederic Augustus Habersham, killed at Fredericksburg.
11. Dickens first published this novel serially in *All the Year Round*, a weekly journal which he established and edited from 1859 to 1870, the year of his death.
12. She had married Seaton Grantland.
13. William Waring Habersham, brother of Josephine.

I taught my children to read and to notice punctuation *while reading*, but that the *most* of it came by nature. A hot day. Read preparatory to Communion next Sunday, an unworthy partaker of this holy feast. A very hot day, but a breeze came up after dinner and we were all sorry that Freddie and the Villalongas[14] did not come out as expected. The table of crabs, finger basins and napkins, and another with fruit, curd and cream all ready, but *nobody came!* Maybe when we are not at all prepared they may come. The afternoon was lovely and pleasant; the grass and trees looked so fresh and green. Anna was bemoaning the lowness of the tide. They were all dressed up, and Babe in his best bib and tucker, but nobody here. However, Mamma and *all* of us went to see Mrs. Tucker. Her place is beautiful, but I really do like ours best—with its open space. She looks like my beloved Sister. William Habersham gone. Robert went in to a Sociable at Saida Elliott's.[15] I told him to ask Jonnie Elliott[16] to come and spend a few days. My Joseph Clay loves him dearly. Paper is so high, I have written between the lines. Neyle gave $100.00 for a barrel of salt fish not long ago and $10.00 for a box of brown sugar yesterday. What prices! $58.00 for a summer muslin. To be sure I bought but *one*. Glad that we had a plenty of material on hand of many kinds and the Nassau[17] trunk of Blockade goods will not soon, I hope give out. Oh! what a treat last night! My good husband came from town *laden* with good things. Said I, "You look as if you had the baby wrapt up there." "Something you like as *well* as the Baby," said he—the scamp—and brought out of a bag the Music and Reviews he asked Mr. Lessing,[18] German pianist, to get. All the English Reviews from January to May, 1863. What a delight! and Books of Haydn's Sonatas, Mozart's

14. John L. Villalonga was a cotton factor and commission merchant. He served as city alderman during the war and later.
15. Daughter of Bishop Stephen Elliott.
16. Saida's brother.
17. There had been a heavy traffic of blockade running between the South Atlantic ports and Nassau, especially during the dark, moonless nights. See Consular dispatches in *Official Records, Navy*, Ser. I, Vol. XIV, pp. 172-173.

Sonatas, and about 30 pieces of flute and piano music. How great a present. My first devout exclamation was, "Oh! may the vile Yankees never *see* them!" My next thought, what a resource in these times of anxiety, such delightful reading, and such noble music. Neyle went in the Bath-house to listen while I played two long Sonatas of Mozart through *at sight* quite nicely. They were tolerable easy, *never so difficult* as Beethoven.

August 8, 1863. Saturday. Have been reading and trying to prepare my wayward heart for the solemnities of the morrow. Not the righteous, but the unrighteous, the unworthy, does the Savior call. Oh! God! make me an *humble* participant, forgetting not that it is of thy Mercy and forbearance I am allowed to approach thy Holy Sacrament.

> The evil of my former state
> Was mine and only mine;
> The good in which I now rejoice
> Is Thine, and only Thine.
>
> Thy grace first made me feel my sin,
> And taught me to believe,
> And in believing, peace I found,
> And now I live, I live.[19]

August 10, 1863. Monday. A very hot day—only the third ,hot day *I've* felt this Summer. They say the thermometer stood 96° at the Pulaski House[20] at two o'clock. A pleasant breeze sprang up this afternoon and I dragged Cherry Cheeks on the Bluff in his little carriage, for he looked very cunningly and lovingly at me, to beg me, and his face all in a glow the moment I took the shaft. Felt dull all day from little désagré-

18. Felix Lessing, a "very charming and accomplished" German pianist. He married Nelly LaRoache of Savannah. Professor Lessing taught Josephine's children and grandchildren, though teaching bored him. He much preferred to accompany Neyle and his famous musician friends in the Thursday evening musicales, which were held at the William Neyle Habersham home on Pulaski Square.
19. This hymn, published in many hymn books since it first appeared, was written by Horatius Bonar in 1856.
20. Hotel in Savannah, facing Johnson Square on the northwest corner of Bull and Congress streets. This old landmark stood until 1957.

mens de la maison. I *ought* to keep up a cheerful spirit, surrounded as I am with so many, many blessings.

We had a very pleasant Sunday service yesterday. Anna King came out to Communion.[21] So that dear Mamma had her two daughters with her. How strange that Mamma should return to the Church and neighborhood where 40 years ago she passed her youth! I trust the services of yesterday may be blessed to my needy spirit.

Heard no lessons today, did not practice—merely read and sewed a little. I was much struck with the lack of interest displayed by the White Bluff people. Nobody at the preparatory meeting! Mamma and I being the *congregation!* Mr. Fulton[22] and Mr. Kieffer,[23] being the Elders. How cold and lukewarm a spirit! But Lord! let me not blame others who know so well the coldness and listlessness of my *own* wayward heart. Mamma was in a perfect fume, of course, because we had to wait nearly half an hour for the Church to be *opened* even! and made herself *hot* with "bother" while I took it coolly and felt delightfully cool waiting in the carriage, during which up came a beautiful rain shower—the raindrops shining through the sun like diamonds.

August 11, 1863. Tuesday. Baby's birthday! One year of the little life which may God spare to be one of usefulness to his fellow creatures, and of happiness and honor to himself, and acceptable to God! His Dah insisted upon a party, so we had a fine watermelon, figs, peaches. Fredericka had made some nice large sponge cakes, and Mr. One Year Old was placed at the table while we drank his health. Mamma's toast with a full heart was "May he live to bless and be blest." *He* drank very eagerly a few drops of wine in water. Grandma gave him a pretty whip, which he uses very fiercely in his carriage. Altogether, it was a happy day!

Reading lately of the persecution of the Jews, particularly in Spain in the fifteenth and sixteenth centuries. To think that

21. The service was at the White Bluff Presbyterian Church.
22. William Fulton.
23. George H. Kieffer.

such a monster as Torquemada[24] ever lived to disgrace the name of Christ—I was about to say—but rather, of the Catholic Religion! One hundred thousand souls did he cause to be put to death, it is estimated.[25] A sentence struck me, "a certain broad equilibrium of their faculties seems to be a Jewish characteristic—*equally remote from febrile enthusiasm, or callous insensibility.*"

We all played with Baby on the Green after dinner.

August 12, 1863. Wednesday. Went to town to see Mary Owens. Got a good likeness of her—a daguerreotype which I've long wanted. Anna King was with me some of the time. She, in the midst of her young family, recalls me to myself when I was surrounded by so many *little* darlings—"a good woman who lives in her shoe." Thank God for the precious baby now mine.

Enjoying the Reviews, the *Blackwood* has a fine piece by an English officer—"A month at Confederate Headquarters."[26] An impartial, truthful account. The writer sees with *Southern* eyes, and denounces the vulgarity and cruelty of Lincoln's cabinet. Gives all due praise to the heroic Stonewall Jackson! Alas! that he should have died. Would that he had lived to share in and witness what *must be our ultimate triumph* as a Nation! And he says Lee is confided in, heart and soul, by the Army, more *reverenced,* as Jackson was *beloved!* and that Lee has the handsomest face he ever saw, and that in a long acquaintance with him he never heard him speak *harshly* of his enemies. A little hate to them would not hurt his Lordship, *I think!* He was rather *Kidglovish* in his invasion of Maryland which, after all, brought so little good!

24. Thomas Torquemada (1420-1498). Intolerant and cruel fanatic who, as Inquisitor-General of Spain, persecuted all non-Catholics and helped to drive out the Jews and Moors during the reign of Ferdinand and Isabella. See Prescott's *History of the Reign of Ferdinand and Isabella* (Boston, 1837, 3 vols.), Vol. 1, ch. 7; Vol. II, ch. 17.
25. This is an exaggeration. The number was more nearly 2,000, but there were fully 100,000 cases of heresy tried, and at least twice that number of Jews were exiled.
26. *Blackwood's Edinburgh Magazine* (Edinburgh, London, 1817-1905), XCIII (1863), 21.

August 13, 1683. Thursday. A delicious day—warm, but a glorious breeze all day. Busy sewing. Practised some of the new music.

Yesterday was anniversary of Robbie Elliott's death. Poor darling Sister Mary![27] And Oh! his sweet young wife! I did not have time to say how much Mary Belle and Lilla enjoyed their drive to town with me, their visit to Mary Owens and Watkin,[28] to Daisy, their *bath*, which made me late at the daguerreotypist's. We got home at *nine* at night. I preferred being late, and the brilliant fireflies entertained us all the way. Lilla and Mary Belle, I was glad to see, were not the least nervous or fussy over the dark drive.

August 14, 1863. Friday. Practised, sewed, read, heard the children's lessons—the days not half long enough for all I would wish to do. Wrote my boy and Willy—t'other boy.

John Rae,[29] Neyle, and Robert went fishing—nice dinner. Played and sang with the children after tea. Delightful breeze all day. Expected Freddie. Sorry they did not come. Had a talk with John about *Les Miserables*. Neyle, he, and I agreed that there are some beauties, some genius and a great deal of folly, absurdity, immorality and nonsense and egotism. What was our exultation to come across a critique in the Quarterly, one of the "Blockade" Reviews, cutting it up most unmercifully, while the *Westminster*,[30] *au contraire*, calls it wonderful, superb and "the masterpiece of the nineteenth Century," allowing, at the same time, that it does nothing toward the moral objects it asserts to write for. Was delighted to turn from its nonsense to a beautiful essay of Bulwer's[31] in *Black-*

27. Robert's mother, not his widow.
28. Mary Wallace Owens' father was Richard N. and George Watkin Owens' father was Col. George S. Their grandfather was George W. Owens, a member of Congress, 1835-1839.
29. John Rae Habersham, Neyle's half-brother.
30. The *Westminster Review* (London, 1824-1914). Its first editor was Sir John Bowring, followed by John Stuart Mill. At this time John Chapman was the editor, though Mary Ann Evans (George Eliot) had carried much of the editorial load.
31. Bulwer-Lytton, Edward George Earle Lytton Bulwer, 1803-1873, English novelist, essayist, dramatist.

wood's. He is a faultless writer, so polished yet so simple. We do really enjoy the Reviews.

August 15, 1863. Saturday. Neyle went to town, but came back in time to receive Captain Brooks[32] at dinner. Had such a nice dinner of home produce, that is *river* produce, fish, turtle, crabs, shrimp, curd, grapes, figs. The Captain seems a good man, kind and pleasant—an *upcountry* man, however![33] He says the Chatham artillery are at James Island. His artillery (Terrell) may have soon to go. Played for him, but he says he often listens on the green! I am afraid our talk in the piazza is often over heard. Robert much interested over Shakespeare. It is a good thing for a young man to see Shakespeare acted well. It gives a taste for all that is manly, noble and refined in mind and beautiful and tender in poetry.

Night. While at dinner read a note from Mr. Manigault telling of the birth of a daughter whom they call "Josephine" after me. Much gratified. I will love the little soul for its parents' sake, its own and in memory of my *two* sweet Josephines—[34] the recollection of my "Sissy" and of Jamesie. Oh! Can I ever lose it?

August 17, 1863. Monday. I forgot to mention what has been entertaining us for several days—our Babe trying to walk! He steps seven or eight steps, bursts out laughing and topples over! Neyle plays with him so much, and does seem to love him as he did our Jamesie! The child recalls him often. Yesterday we were all amused by Captain Brooks bringing *me* two *elegant* peaches as we stood before tea on the piazza. They were sent him from Columbus; but *the joke* was that Dr. Bonner, to whom Captain Brooks had given some, had just brought me one! Forestalled him. I laughed at Anna that I was preferred to her, but she determined to immortalize it, for she planted the stones with a great piece of board marked, "Captain Brooks, Terrell Artillery, August, 1863."

32. Captain John W. Brooks, appointed Lieutenant of Terrell Light Artillery, Sept. 27, 1861.
33. Here Josephine reflects the typical Tidewater attitude toward the people of the hinterland.
34. Her own children who died young.

August 18, 1863. Tuesday. Very heavy rain—very dark and cool. Practised, heard the children their lessons, read the Reviews, wrote J. C.

August 19, 1863. Wednesday. Rain all day. Played a great deal with Cherry Cheeks, who is walking with help. The little bare feet will have to have shoes. Neyle staid out two days because of bad weather. The figs pretty much over. Neyle is now petting me up with grapes. Bombarding at the Forts as usual. Heard 14 heavy cannon, but we never mind them now. Read Reviews. Lilla getting on so well in Grammar. Fine letter from J. C. by General Johnston. How I wish our boy could be at home. He says he longs for a "smoke of cigar with Pa in the Piazza." Willie came from Augusta where he had a fine time. Looked extremely well. Willie went to Rose Dew [*sic*], and brought home Hunter and May to tea. Played first with children, and then with Neyle 'till 10 o'clock. Practising the new music. Read Reviews. Rainy day.

August 20, 1863. Thursday. Neyle and Robert came out to dinner. Practised and sewed. Played with Babe a long time after dinner. He loves me most of all. How the children do love him! and as to Papa! Mamma busy making a lovely tucked dress for Fanny's "Josephine," fine work for a lady of 67 years! Mine she made for Baby was beautifully made. Neyle and Robert gone fishing this splendid afternoon. We are to go to Hover's[35] to buy pears. Baby seems to understand "he is to go to ride in Mamma's carriage." Made every sign as if he knew. Tomorrow is *Fast Day.*

Night. We had a delightful drive to Hover's. Edward enjoyed every moment—we all did. I always envy Mr. Hover the lovely cedars when I go there. All the pears gone. Bombarding very heavy on the Islands, and Parrott guns from the *new* Battery on Morris Island affect Sumpter [*sic*] much. People begin to fear that Sumpter [*sic*] may fall. The guns from the South (sea) side do not return fire. All quiet in Mississippi and with Lee's Army.[36] Bragg still.[37]

August 21, 1863. Friday. Fast Day. Did not feel well

---

35. A store at nearby Montgomery on the Vernon River.

enough to go to Church. Tried to humble myself in private before Almighty God as an unworthy sinner should do before "Him in whose sight, the very Heavens are not clean." All went to Church but I; Neyle and Anna went to hear Cousin Stephen.[38] Neyle brought me the previous Sunday's sermon (Bishop Elliott's), a very solemn call on *all* to humble themselves and repent before God, that his hand and his wrath might not be hard upon us. Pretty dull news of Sumpter [*sic*], does not return fire! and papers begin to talk of the safety of Charleston not *depending* on Sumter. Alas! What a pity if the Yankees should have the triumph of humbling Sumter! There is great prestige connected with that Fort. Sitting in the piazza with Neyle, Grandma on the green with Baby in her arms see-sawing when Mr. Cumming[39] and Major Gibbons[40] called. Major Gibbons has just returned from Charleston, and says people were not discouraged about Sumter.

August 22, 1863. Saturday. Hot in the morning, and heaviest kind of rain, mid-day. The gentlemen, John Rae, Gillie Wilkins, Willy and Robert went fishing. Caught a *plenty* for nice dinner. Glad to have piano as a resource when too dark to do anything else, and entertained the company. Lilla and I played pretty duets—I making bass to her really good, excellent treble. Anna and I find *Great Expectations* pretty hard to read—so foolish. Wrote my dear Joseph Clay.

36. After Gettysburg (July 3), Lee returned to Virginia and settled down on the Rapidan to bring his army to offensive strength again, saying, "We must now prepare for harder blows." But it became apparent that it would be impossible to do so at least in the immediate weeks ahead. See Douglas Southall Freeman, *R. E. Lee; A Biography* (New York, 1934-1935, 4 vols.), III, 162-164.
37. Bragg could not be "still" much longer because Rosecrans would force him out of Chattanooga by Sept. 9. See *Official Records, War,* Ser. I, Vol. XX, pt. 2, p. 22.
38. Bishop Stephen Elliott, first Episcopal bishop of Georgia. The Bishop's mother, Esther Habersham, was the daughter of James, of the second Georgia generation of Habershams. Neyle and Anna went in to town to Christ Church to hear the Bishop preach.
39. Montgomery Cumming was agent for William Heyward Gibbons, who owned the Whitehall plantation. The Gibbons family later moved to New Jersey. See Writers' Program, Georgia, *Savannah River Plantations* (Savannah, 1947), 318, 321-330.
40. Maj. Gibbons was in home defense.

So sorry not to get to Isle of Hope to see my dear brother, Dr. J. C., just returned, sick, from James Island. Tom[41] was busy. Must go next week. Felt dull and tired, out of spirits. Came to bed early.

August 23, 1863. Sunday. Mamma gone to Isle of Hope to see dear brother J. C. Oh! I hope he is not seriously sick. Mary Anna sent for Mamma and she says she feels worried about him. All went to Church. Dear Babe seems more and more fond of me. Wish dear Dr. J. C., who loves him so much, could see him walking and laughing out. The little girls delighted to get some Sunday books to read from Aunt Belle C.[42] Telegram is that they are *shelling* Charleston from Craig's Hill! Everything quiet in Mississippi and Virginia. Received a nice, entertaining letter from Joseph Clay—Merton, Mississippi.

> Not in anger smite us, Lord!
> Spare they people, spare!
> If thou mete us due reward
> We must all despair.
>
> Let the flood
> Of Jesus' blood
> Quench the flaming of thy wrath,
> That our sin unkindled hath.

August 24, 1863. Monday. While sitting in my room, after hearing the children's lessons, dull enough, thinking of brother J. C.'s sickness, in come the newspapers from town, "Sumter in ruins!"[43] Colonel Rhett[44] ordered to hold it, until relieved, with his brave garrison." General Gilmore [*sic*] threatens to shell Charleston today at 11 o'clock. Beauregard answers "uncivilized and inhuman conduct" to allow no time to the

---

41. Her coachman.
42. Isabelle Charlotte, her father's sister.
43. Major-General Quincy A. Gillmore, U. S. A., commanding the Department of the South, opened fire at daybreak on the 17th and reported the "particial demolition" of the fort on the 24th. *Official Records, War*, Ser. I, Vol. XXVIII, pt. 1, pp. 598-99.
44. Colonel Alfred Rhett was relieved by Major Stephen Elliott, Jr., on Sept. 5 and sporadic bombardment continued. *Ibid.*, 608. The demolished fort was not surrendered until Feb., 1865. See Randall, *op. cit.*, 591.

inhabitants. No answer returned as yet! Non combatants leaving Charleston. Oh! what a state of things! Another paper says "a Mexican lady, wealthy, whose husband offered to pay her weight in silver if let free, was sentenced to receive 200 lashes for not entertaining French officers!" The French rule everything now in Mexico.[45] This done by a General of *the most refined* and civilized of nations! What are we coming to! I dashed the paper down, and cried with sheer mortification! What is to be expected of the dastardly Yankees after that! And *these things they do!* Good God! I would rather die, I and my little ones, than be in *the power* of these wretches. Neyle gone to town. I feel too wretched.

August 25, 1863. Tuesday. Went today to Isle of Hope with the three little girls[46] to see my dear brother, Dr. J. C. With a most thankful heart, I say we found him better—looking thin and badly, but much better—and will perhaps now do very well. Ordinary fever Dr. George says. Poor fellow. Such repeated attacks as he has had, since they have been located in unhealthy spots. He will have to rest now, and, indeed, he was too unwell to have returned to James Island; had fever all the time. Nothing but a sense of duty made him stay. This consciousness is what will make a weary heart and body happy. We had a pleasant day, they begged us to stay to dinner, but I wanted to return. Mamma much relieved about Joseph Clay. Florence[47] begged us hard to stay to dinner. The papers which Neyle brought out informed us of the shameful shelling of Charleston without warning the inhabitants. Gillmore seems to be a vagabond. "Sumter in ruins," but still holding out. Several formidable Batteries yet to be overcome before they can take Charleston, though they may shell it. Have heard twice from Mr. Manigault since

45. Napoleon III, taking advantage of the war in the United States, had sent into Mexico a French army which occupied Mexico City on June 7, 1863. On April 10, 1864, he placed Archduke Maximilian of Austria on the throne as Emperor of Mexico.
46. Anna, 14; Lilla, 10; and Mary Belle, 9.
47. Florence Stiles, sister of Mary Anna. Mary Anna was the wife of Dr. Joseph Clay Habersham, Josephine's brother. Florence married Wylly Woodbridge.

little *Josephine* was born, and have written him twice. Wrote a long letter to Fannie Bolton Habersham.[48] On the way home, the fifth wheel broke, and we had to get out while Tom got assistance from a picket camp near, and with board and rope we got home. Carriage gone to town today to be mended. We had no *passport,* but they allowed us to pass. A rain pelted in the carriage on Mary Belle for ten minutes, but our nice Asquascutums protected her thoroughly. We had fine fun. Anna had to laugh, with her ear-ache. Poor child! she had it all day, and put her head in my lap driving home.

August 26, 1863. Wednesday. Willy took Gillie Wilkins in last night. A heavy rain again. Sorry that Scipio is interrupted taking the grass from the garden and manuring the roses. Dear Babe played beautifully today, rolling a sour orange which he picked himself off the tree! I wonder if the soldiers will let the hundreds we have ripen! Robert is getting a wetting this minute, off fishing. I do *wonder* they never have fever. Wetting really seems to do *Willy* good—it certainly don't harm him. Getting Joseph Clay's things ready to send, have put aside some nice "tin cans" for him, recalling the time when he and John[49] had had nothing to eat for two days, and poor water, and he sent John to a Hospital to beg for two biscuits, and just as they got them his baggage came up, and there was the herring paste I had put up in his valise, saying at the time, "Dear boy, I'll put this in *here* because you can get it sometime when you are tired and hungry." Tired and hungry he was, and *wet* and very thankful, as he wrote, for Mamma's "usual kind thoughtfulness and care." They said *never was there such a feast* as that herring and begged biscuits! Lilla complaining to-day of headache from the long drive yesterday—always disagrees with her.

August 27, 1863. Thursday. How this Summer is passing! And so little hot weather. Surely not more than four hot nights! and already the weather is chilly at times. Practised a

48. She was Frances Hazlehurst and had married John Bolton Habersham, Josephine's brother. They lived in Brunswick.
49. Joseph Clay's body servant.

long time, the new pieces, flute and piano. Sang. My voice is stronger again. Read the Reviews, and am *trying* to finish *Great Expectations*. A lovely Fall morning, but heavy rains after dinner. Neyle and Robert came to dinner through pouring rains, but Asquascutums kept them dry. After dinner we *all* went crabbing, far off. Had a fine, pleasant time. Sun under a splendid cloud, immense, and like a wide spread dark banner *fringed* with silver, so exactly did the jagged edges of light represent silver. Lilla and I rowed home. I felt like a girl again when I used to row often and well. Anna beats me now, *with* tide, of course, we were. Neyle wants me to row *every day* to "expand my chest!" which has no fault of *narrowness*, I'm sure! Had music after tea. We keep up our spirits as well as we can. A nice letter from dear J. C. No recent bombarding of Charleston. Assault on Fort Wagner *repulsed*. Great talks of Yankee raids into Georgia, etc.

August 28, 1863, Friday. Went to Sam Stiles' this lovely fall morning to bring Mamma home from Isle of Hope. Was not there. Dear brother J. C. is really better, thank God! We started in the Carryall, with bright skies. The rain began to *pour just* as we got there. Baby looked very strange at Sam Stiles. Poor Sam must feel lonely without Carrie.[50] He spoke of her with tears, and I could not but weep, for I liked and admired her much. On the way home we stopped in the "Big Field" to see Terrell Artillery practise. I saw several shots—Black Hawk[51] not at all alarmed, nor *baby*. A hard rain, too, came up exactly as at Sam's *just* as we arrived at our door. Such a rain! in which Willy and Marion Morrell and two Cohen girls were caught. They had *nothing* to protect *them*, careless girls, so Willie's coats and blankets did *them* service, and not *him*. He was *drenched*. Rain poured all afternoon. Very chilly. Glad to have my books and music. We got off Joseph Clay's package by George Johnston, a *nice* parcel, and his kind Papa sent handsome boots, bridle, etc., etc., all of which cost a plenty—$50.00 for the bridle. Sumter still held,

50. Sam V. Stiles had married Caroline Rogers who had died.
51. Joseph Clay's horse.

although in ruins. It did not reply to forts, and when Monitors came by, opened on *them*, showing all was not *dead*. They had to retreat. Bad news—the enemy surprised our picket and captured our rifle pits 400 yards from Fort Wagner! Morris Island will have to *go* probably. A letter from Louis Manigault says the family are with them.

Read Shakespeare first time for a fortnight, I believe. The days are not half long enough for all I want to do, for I must teach and read with my children, play with Baby, etc., etc. Our dear boy ordered to Tennessee with Walker's Division.[52] *He* is glad! Can *I* tell, poor me, whether to be glad or *sorry?* God only knows! I try to place my child freely in His hands, but oh! the wearying anxiety! General Lee's position and locality is kept secret.[53] Robert brought Habby Elliott[54] out last night.

August 29, 1863. Saturday. A most lovely fall day. I busy myself with *trimming* up, etc. Practised a long time, Mozart. Heard Anna practise. Boys and Neyle fishing all day, caught 150 crabs. Baby learning so many new tricks, and would walk well if only he had a pair of soled shoes. He loves me more and more. How thankful I am that my darling is so well— only has a boil or two while teething. Read Reviews and sewed, too. Beautiful piece on the life of Rubens, painter.

August, 30, 1863. Sunday. Went to Church, all of us. Heavy rain set in.

Our dear Robert's birthday—17 years. God grant he may always be to his parents the good child he now is! Little Daisy came home with us from Church. Anna King and family coming out tomorrow as little Joseph Clay[55] is very

52. "We know that Bragg had been re-enforced by troops sent by Johnston from Mississippi. . . ." Halleck's report, Nov. 15, 1863, in *Official Records, War*, Ser. I, Vol. XXX, pt. 1, p. 38.
53. In August Lee's army was somewhere on the Rapidan, and at the end of the month Lee himself went to Richmond at the request of President Davis to discuss the problems of desertion, shortage of corn for the horses, and general strategy. He left Longstreet in charge and did not return until Sept. 7. See Freeman, *Lee*, III, 163-164.
54. Habersham Elliott.
55. Here is the fourth Joseph Clay! First, there was Josephine's father, then her brother, next her son, now her sister Anna Wylly's child.

unwell. So glad to have my dear Sister with us! The children answered their Bible questions beautifully, sang hymns. Very chilly fall weather.

August 31, 1863. Monday. Rainy and chilly. Sewed, taught and read all day. Practised an hour—left hand. So glad to see the servants working at the flower garden once more, nothing but *greenery* now, and a very pretty one. Wrote to Mr. Higham for Bishop's sermon I lent him on strength under affliction. It is good to read sometimes to strengthen the faith for actual or *probable* evils.

Sumter still holding out, although a ruin. Bragg expecting a fight from Rosencranz.[56] My boy must be there now, near Chattanooga. Glad Johnston took his blankets, etc. Must try in the quiet of today to read my Shakespeare. Batteries at Charleston under *continued* assault, but Morris Island will probably have to be given up to the Yankees.

Brother J. C. better—down stairs. *I'm thankful.* His loss would be irreparable. Wrote Louis Manigault. A pleasant letter from our boy—the *last*, he hopes, from Mississippi. The Tennessee field is more healthy. Only one or two sick men now in Camp here, and I try to send something each day. Potatoes are $1.00 a quart—seven [potatoes]. Read Reviews till late. Quite cold.

56. The big fight did not take place until Sept. 19-20, when the Confederates defeated the Yankees at Chickamauga. See next chapter.

"*His horse is slain, and all on foot he fights,
Seeking for Richmond in the throat of death.*"
—Shakespeare, *Richard the Third*

TEARS IN THEIR EYES

The storm over the Potomac rolled southward, and the angry war clouds over the Mississippi moved eastward until the two storm areas joined at Chattanooga. But the tide of Southern hope surged upward briefly at Chickamauga and news of the Confederate victory is pleasant to hear. It brings joy to Avon, but Josephine's anxiety increases as she learns that her son's horse has been shot from under him. Neyle said there was no cause for crying, but his own eyes were wet.

September 1, 1863. Tuesday. The Summer is over! Have I improved it as I should have done? Have I improved my children? Let me put these questions to myself in the privacy of my room, and ask God's forgiveness that I am not a *more faithful* servant.

Going to send to Isle of Hope for Mamma. Anna King prevented coming out by bad cold weather.

September 2, 1683. Wednesday. Glad to hear my dear brother is better, but quite sick. Was writing this *lovely* morning to my dear boy when my Sister Anna and all her little family arrived. Her fine Baby does not look well—fretful from teething. Little delicate Joseph Clay looks wretchedly indeed. I hope the change will do him good. She reminds me of the time when *I* had my hands full of young ones! I should love *never* to be without a sweet baby to mind, care for and love.

Music in the evening. Mary Belle singing in such a spirited way.

September 3, 1863. Thursday. Anna and Mary gone to town—the latter to put up my velvet cloak which has become damp from hanging up, and to bring some fall things for the children. Phenie Wayne[1] and Colonel Hartridge[2] came over to take Anna back with them. I will get her father to send her to Rose Dew [sic] tomorrow to spend the day. Snatched a little time to read *Troilus and Cressida*. Not much done but playing and holding babies, as Anna's two children both want to be with her all the time. Nothing new from Charleston or Tennessee. Charles King enjoyed his fishing much.

September 4, 1863. Friday. Not much else done than talking, looking after babies, etc. Anna went to spend the day with Phenie Wayne at Rose Dew [sic]; Baby, Dinah, and Mabelle going with her in the Carryall. In the afternoon Anna King, Lilla, and I went in the carriage for her. Mrs. Hartridge and all and I went over to the Battery over a beautiful Causeway and a handsome, I mean strong, bridge. There is a beautiful Battery, so covered with verdure, four rifle guns. We went into the dark, excessively *hot* Magazine (with a lantern) where the 120-pound *shells* ranged on the shelves looked like skulls as if it were a Golgotha. How it must exhaust the men to be in these bombproofs, of a hot stifling day with all the miserable accompaniments of a bombardment—wounds, death, perhaps *worse*, disaster and defeat. Dr. Bonner (Terrell Artillery) came to tea. I sent soup to the Hospital today, and asking after them, he sends me a list of sick—names and ailments—so that I may know what to send. He is so *still*, although not stupid. Why can't he talk? Admired our music. A letter from our boy, Chickamauga, Tennessee[3]—quite well, and all baggage safe.

September 5, 1863. Saturday. A lovely day. Dear little Louis' birthday, five years old.[4] One would think him seven years. Must write my child. Finished *Troilus and Cressida*. Don't like it any better than before. There are a few fine expressions (became proverbial) and a great deal of fine

1. She later married Louis Warfield.
2. Col. Alfred Lamar Hartridge was on Brig.-Gen. Hugh Weedon Mercer's staff.
3. She is mistaken. Chickamauga is in Georgia, near the Tennessee line.
4. Child of Louis and Frances Manigault.

language among the Greek and Trojan Chiefs, but not much interest and a great many disagreeable things. *Very* carefully composed. Must write letters this lovely day. Willy gone to town for the day; Robert, Habby, and Neyle fishing.

September 6, 1863. Sunday. All went to Church. A good Sermon about our being Prisoners of Hope. Must fly to the stronghold for safety. Charles set the hymns so low that nobody could sing. I love dearly to sing in Church; hearing so little,[5] I have to take what part I *may* in the Services. Charles came to dinner, found his two children better. Received a note from Mr. Higham, and a most valuable present of two Belmontine *wax* candles—beautiful. Will use them to read by. Wrote my dear boy.

September 7, 1863. Monday. All well—Anna's children better. We all sang hymns last night, Willy's loud voice joined in. News from the Islands more decided. Anna gone for the day to Montgomery. Willy, Robert, and Habby gone to 'Possum to fish. Tom reports no meat, and not a chicken to be had in market this morning! I had a chicken for the soldiers, but had to *draw in*. Finished *Pericles* last week. The story is pretty and interesting, but I don't particularly like that play, and some parts are dreadfully indelicate. Really must *practise* more. I sometimes wish I could be in town at a soldiers' prayer meeting. Think I will go in on Wednesdays sometimes.

September 8, 1863. Tuesday. Last night played Beethoven and Mozart with Neyle, mostly *at sight*. Sad news! Batteries Gregg and Wagner[6] evacuated! But it was necessary as the enemy *mined* so near, and such a furious bombardment was opened from so short a distance! So Morris Island is given up![7] Happily all the men escaped, which is wonderful; in 40 Barges, except one boat of 12 men captured. I feared, or the community did, that *many hundreds* would be captured. A

5. Josephine's deafness increased as she grew older.
6. Fort Wagner and Battery Gregg were in Charleston harbor.
7. See Col. William Butler's report, Sept. 12, in *Official Records, Navy*, Ser. I, Vol. XIV, pp. 577-578.

really handsome letter, very long and interesting, from dear J. C., Chickamauga. Heard all the children their lessons today. They improve in French, and Anna improves in Music. Anna King's little ones quite bright. How I wish she lived near me here! Mamma would be more contented, too. Wrote a long letter to my boy. Lilla played for us the most of the evening 'till it got so late that we sat and talked out the evening. So sorry my dear Sister goes tomorrow.[8]

September 9, 1863. Wednesday. Dear Anna and family went this morning. Had a very pleasant visit, and little children improved. Charles King was much pleased with Lilla and Mary Belle in their *French*—by memory only. Heard Anna her lessons *thoroughly.* We are at English and French Grammar, I hope to get her well "grounded" before she begins school again, as the teachers are so careless. Much time is taken up in the news of the day, Savannah, Charleston, and Richmond papers. Morris Island lost to us, and we hear that about 30 men were captured, but the enemy is not much nearer the conquest of Charleston for all that. There has been *an assault,* in barges, on *Sumter, repulsed.* Two *Monitors* have been injured. Katana writes from Roswell[9] of an alarm. Everybody packed up in the night. Companies out, but scouts returned saying they (the enemy) had been driven back. My Joseph Clay is at Rome, Georgia, Gist's Brigade sent there in a hurry. Gist in command there,[10] and J. C. is extremely busy. So sorry that Captain Gist,[11] whom J. C. nursed in Mississippi, is dead. J. C. says he was a Christian, and "more fit to die than any of the Staff." He seems to feel his death.

8. Anna King and her children had been visiting at Avon for a week and two days.
9. There was a skirmish near Roswell Sept. 11th. See report of Maj.-Gen. Thomas L. Crittenden (U. S. A.), Oct. 1, 1863, in *Official Records, War,* Ser. I, Vol. XXX, pt. 1, p. 603.
10. See report of Brig.-Gen. S. R. Gist (C. S. A.), Oct. 14, 1863 in *Official Records, War,* Ser. I, Vol. XXX, pt. 2, pp. 244-247.
11. Probably William M. Gist, listed on first muster roll of Co. B, 15th Regiment, S. C. Infantry (Sept. 6, 1861), as Captain, age 20. This company was mustered into service Aug. 22, 1861. No evidence of his being related to Gen. S. R. Gist. S. C. Archives Dept., Columbia, S. C.

Dear Babe can "pat-a-cake" when you tell him, and learns something new every day. Lilla and Mary Belle and Anna enjoy so much taking him on the green in his carriage. A hurried note from J. C. from Rome. I wrote him a long letter yesterday. We all sang tonight all the songs we have, joined by Willie May,[12] Willie, Robert. Had *grand times!* Made noise enough! I *love* to sing with my children.

The papers say that the enemy's "parallels" have approached so near to Wagner that our fire could not be distinguished from the enemy's! Immense Parrott guns at a little distance. The sand hills where the wounded lay were exposed to fire. Before they left the dead were buried and matches applied to blow up the forts, but, alas! they did not explode! Guns were spiked, etc., etc. It was all well done it seems.

Oh! to think that a fight may come off at any moment where my dear boy is! God bless him!

The sick at Hospital much pleased today at soup and wine Sangaree I sent them.

September 10, 1863. Thursday. Dr. J. C. and Mary Anna came. My dear brother is weak and thin, but looks better than I expected to see him. Delighted with Baby and his winning ways. He stares very hard at them. News of the evacuation of Batteries Gregg and Wagner that it was a *complete success*, done so quietly, conducted by Harry Bryan of Savannah.[13] Georgia does well when tried. Dear old Georgia! She never did bluster, as South Carolina has done, but does her duty. North Carolina seems to be treacherous—the majority. An assault on poor ruined Sumter was *repulsed.* Not one killed on our side! Several officers (18), three fine barges, four colors,[14] and 210 men captured, and the old Federalist flag

---

12. William H. May, Willie's friend, was a native of Connecticut. In Savannah he entered the saddle and harness business. He died in 1884.
13. She must have meant Major Henry Bryan whom Gen. Ripley commended in his report of Aug. 21. See *Official Records, Navy*, Ser. I, Vol. XIV, p. 744.
14. Banners, or flags. This could mean the flags of the barges or company standards.

which Anderson carried away,[15] which they brought back to *replace in triumph*, was also captured. The glory of the day, or night, is great, but alas! they are so *many* that poor Sumter may yet become theirs!

September 11-12, 1863. Friday and Saturday. Much occupied in entertaining Mary Anna and J. C. A beautiful, lively letter from my boy. Many things make me feel dull. I am glad to play with my babe who loves me more and more. He can pat-a-cake! and has many winning ways.

September 13, 1863. Sunday. All went to Church. Church full, many soldiers. Stopped to see the sick soldier in our small house on the road. He is very ill, and thankful for the mattress I sent him, poor fellow! He and *his* wife lying on thin old counterpanes. Have sent wine Sangaree to the sick at Hospital. Mrs. Tucker is so good to them, has some at her house now. She makes good use of her big fine house. We all sang hymns this evening. Dear Babe seems never to tire of "See-saw." I really get tired first. Only to think of the enemy so near! We learn that Longstreet has reinforced Bragg, or is on the way. Unfortunate occurrence, the big gun in Charleston has burst!

September 18, 1863. Friday. All this week I have been quite indisposed, although not in bed but two days.[16] We have had much rainy and cool weather. Two letters from our dear boy in Rome, Georgia, where they are quiet at present. A young lady had sent him a pillow, learning he had no such luxury, with *two* linen pillowcases! He is happy in being *in a house* and having a real bed. Writes in fine spirits. Rosencranz will hardly have time to fortify himself very strongly in Chattanooga if all I hear is right—as the idea is that Bragg will fight *at once.* How anxious I feel! God

15. On Apr. 12, 1861, Charleston shore batteries under the command of Gen. Beauregard opened fire on the Federal Fort Sumter, forcing Maj. Robert Anderson and his garrison to surrender it. Thus began the war. The Federals had practically demolished the fort the week of Aug. 17-24, 1863, but the Confederacy did not surrender it until Feb., 1865. The flag to which Josephine referred was finally placed over the ruins of Fort Sumter on April 14, 1865, in a Union Victory ceremony.

16. This is the second gap in the diary. See July 25.

preserve my child, who does his duty manfully. Have been reading *Aurora Floyd*[17]—well written and interesting, but too *sensational*, too dramatic, and the events follow one another in too *quick time*. Read *Two Gentlemen of Verona*—interesting and some parts extremely well written, some beautiful thoughts. Of course I have often read it before. Also, *Comedy of Errors*, which I never liked much, but *of course* it is Shakespeare's. I don't see *why* it should be doubted. Schlegel[18] says finely of *Two Gentlemen of Verona*—"It is as if the whole world was obliged to accommodate itself to a transient caprice called love."

Dear Baby loves me more and more, wants to be with me all the time, understands nearly all that's said to him. Mary Wylly staying with Anna. She suffers from Tooth ache.

September 19, 1863. Saturday. Took a long walk with Mamma and children this really cool day. Practised, sewed, wrote Joseph Clay. Wrote Mr. Higham on Friday afternoon a Shakespearian letter—for such they have always been—to send by Robert who went to spend today with him.

No further news except that *our* batteries fire on Morris Island, fire not returned and that the *other* big gun, our great hope, sank in the mud off the trestle of the car and can't be removed, after running the blockade safely from England through a watchful enemy's fleet!

And Bragg is fronting Rosencranz[19] and no further com-

17. A novel by Mary Elizabeth Braddon (Mrs. John Maxwell). Two American editions of this English novel appeared in 1863, one by Harper & Bros., and another by a Richmond publisher, West & Johnson. Miss Braddon also wrote *Lady Audley's Secret.*
18. August Wilhelm Schlegel, best of German translators of Shakespeare, along with his brother, Friedrich, and Ludwig Tieck.
19. On this very day the two-day Battle of Chickamauga began. Joseph Clay's division commander, Maj.-Gen. W. H. T. Walker, was erroneously reported among the more than 2,000 Confederates killed ("Passing over the field, we found the dead body of General Walker." Report of Lt. Col. Frank Erdelmyer, 32nd Indian Infantry, U. S. A., in *Official Records, War*, Ser. I, Vol. XXX, pt. 1, pp. 546-547). He was killed the next year in the Battle of Atlanta (July 22, 1864). Joseph Clay was not hit, but his horse was shot from under him (see entry of Sept. 22).

munication is at present to be held with the rear. So I shall miss for a time the comfort of my boy's frequent letters.

Saturday night. A long letter from our boy, who leaves Rome. Where to go he could not tell. I must direct [my letters] to Atlanta. We played the new music; most of it *at sight.*

September 20, 1863. Sunday. A really cold day. Willy brought Willy May home last evening from the Cohens, and he is quite sick today. Went yesterday to see the sick men. Those in Hospital are quite comfortable, seemed thankful to us Ladies for the nice things sent. A lovely cold day. My darling Sissy's anniversary of *death* passed while I was so unwell last week, 17th. Shall I ever forget her sweet face as she lay covered with roses and flowers and snowberries in that room in Boston.[20] She would be 21 years her next birthday, December 4! What a sweet and lovely memory is hers!

September 21, 1863. Monday. A bright clear day, beautiful—too bright for my anxious heart. Heard the children's lessons. Lilla and Mary Belle do admirably in French phrases. I am touching Anna up in her English Grammar and French *Verbs*—getting along pretty well. Willy May continues quite sick. We can have no music. Took a long delightful walk with the children. Busy sewing all day.

September 22, 1863. Tuesday. Mamma got a note from Anna King saying her brother Tom was *killed* in battle of Ringgold,[21] near Chattanooga. Poor Mother, and wife, and father! Three sweet children left. Oh! how anxious I felt about our darling, but I received a short letter from him dated *just before the battle* saying he never felt so enthusiastic. So affectionate and considerate in him to write. Then I felt anxious still. Anna and Mamma had gone in to town (*they*

20. "Sissy" was Josephine's daughter Josephine Elizabeth, who died of pneumonia in 1852 at ten years of age. She was with her parents who were visiting friends in Boston.
21. Skirmish, Sept. 17, See *Official Records, War,* Ser. I, Vol. XXX, pt. 1, p. 859. She meant her brother-in-law, Tom King, of Roswell, Ga. This skirmish preceded the Battle of Chickamauga, but is considered a part of it.

brought the letter). Neyle came out with Robert, late to tea, and put a telegram from the dear child on my plate—"I am safe, but my horse was shot under me." Thank God for his safety! Oh! *Am* I not grateful! A solemn sense of gratitude fills my heart. The eyes at table were not dry. Mamma and I cried outright. Neyle said there was no cause for crying, but his *own eyes* were wet. Oh! how anxious I feel! Trying to throw off my care. I and the little girls took a delightful walk away to the Shell Road, and got many wild flowers. Stopped to see the sick men, who are better. Dr. Bonner and Dr. Wilson both called to see Willy May. He has much fever. Baby *cries in fun* so prettily, and points with his fingers at pictures, and sometimes looks at his fingers a long time, talking to himself. So glad to hear that dear Joseph Clay is well again.

September 23, 1863. Wednesday. Wrote my dear boy, although I can't tell *when* he will get it. Sorry his horse called "Robert Beverley," is shot—a present from his father.

Willy and his friend May went to town today. We fixed May nicely upon two mattresses, with pillows and Willie's red cap (smoking). He looked quite interesting. I hope he will improve under Dr. Arnold's care.[22] We felt anxious about him out here.

News from Bragg's Army. The victory, he says, is *complete*,[23] about 4,000 prisoners captured and much artillery, etc. Longstreet and Hill are after the enemy in their *retreat* to the *mountains*. All of Rosencranz's Army was engaged. Numbers greatly superior to *ours*. This victory is a Godsend so far!

22. Dr. Richard Arnold, prominent Savannah physician, who served five one-year terms as mayor of the city between 1842 and 1865.
23. The Confederates, under Bragg assisted by Longstreet and A. P. Hill, routed Rosecrans and chased the Federals back into Tennessee following their victory at Chickamauga, Sept. 20. Thomas held for awhile— long enough to earn the sobriquet "Rock of Chickamauga"—but then he, too, followed the other divisions back to Chattanooga. Bragg was jubilant. He wrote to Gen. Cooper, "The victory is complete"; and to his men he said, "Trusting in God and the justice of our cause, and nerved by the love of dear ones at home, failure is impossible, and victory must be ours." *New York Times*, Sept. 25, 1863.

Pray God we may follow it up.[24] Rosencranz left the field covered with his dead,[25] but we, also, lost many men and many officers.

September 24, 1863. Thursday. Mr. Higham came and brought a note from our dear boy—*after* the battle. He says his horse was killed at the very first of the battle, and he fought on foot—"all afoot," like Richard III. He says he did his *duty.* I know he did. God bless him and make me grateful for his safety. Mr. Higham played, of course, and made *me* play. Took a walk in the afternoon, and saw an *elegant* sunset! The reflection in the river was lovely—"Sweet Vesper's pageant."[26] Music at night. Lilla pleased Mr. Higham by playing a piece she composed—very pretty and accurate. The little girls are glad to see some new books from town. Dear Baby looks so fat, and is so good and sweet. Cares for nothing so much as being with me. Things quiet at Charleston. Batteries *playing,* as usual. Nothing very new from Bragg's Army except that he has had a *press correspondent* arrested in Rome.[27] Neyle wrote to J. C.

September 25, 1863.[28] *Friday.* Neyle and all gone fishing. Busy practising. My thumb hurts me from a cedar thorn—can't sew. Mr. Higham quite unwell, mopes about.

September 26, 1863. Saturday. A lovely day, out nearly all day with the children. Weather too tempting to stay *in.* Neyle and Robert went fishing. Anna to Montgomery to spend the day. The child is so fond of Mary.[29] Indeed, she

---

24. But it was not to be. "All that had been achieved at Chickamauga had been undone." Freeman, *Lee,* III, 206. After his defeat at Lookout Mountain and Missionary Ridge, Nov. 23-25, Bragg was relieved of command and Lt.-Gen. W. J. Hardee was given temporary command of the Army of Tennessee. Later, Johnston succeeded him. See *Official Records, War,* Ser. I, Vol. XXXI, pt. 2, p. 682.
25. See Trowbridge's description of the disinterment of the dead. Gordon Carroll, ed., *The Desolate South, 1865-1866,* by John T. Trowbridge (Boston, 1956), 137-39.
26. Here she twists Antony's lines to suit her own mood. "They are black Vesper's pageants." *Antony and Cleopatra,* IV. 14. 8.
27. The reason for this is not known. Actually, censorship was not strictly enforced generally.
28. Josephine dated it the 24th.

loves a companion at all times. Neyle and I practised after tea the new music after singing with the children.

September 27, 1863. Sunday. Yesterday was the birthday of my dear sweet little baby Josephine Vernon. A silver cup of hers and her tomb-stone with the rosebuds (designed by dear Sister Mary Ann) are nearly all that tells of her short life, but I do not forget the pretty little creature whom I nourished for her short life at my breast. No Church as Charles has gone to Roswell[30] to see his afflicted family. Wrote my boy on Saturday, and Emma Habersham.[31] Sang hymns after tea with the children. Sat with little Lilla after dinner, who had eaten too many ground-nuts and was unwell.

September 28, 1863. Monday. Took a long walk with Mr. Higham after practising. Dear Lilla much better. No news from Bragg or Charleston.

September 29, 1863. Tuesday.[32] Heard the children's lessons, practised, sewed. Took a drive to Sam Stiles' with baby and children. Long letter from our boy, and wrote to him. How much they suffer from hunger. No dinner—a little biscuit, hard and old, a slice of bacon, *sometimes*. Two chickens and a plate of biscuit for eleven hungry men was the gratest dinner they've had for one week! After marching 17 miles, a hard fight all day, and one biscuit at night! But the child does not complain! He rejoices in being one of those who fought for our rights *on*, and drove the enemy *from*, our *own soil!* One letter contained a clear diagram of the battle.

September 30, 1863. Wednesday. Went to town with Mamma to see John Bolton.[33] Went last night over to the Constantines' house[34] to see the dancing party, taking the children. I did not care to send Anna without me, and went,

29. Mary Newell, one of her best friends. Other good friends of Anna were Katana King, Mamie and Jennie Cohen, Phenie Wayne, and Sallie Schley.
30. Twenty miles north of Atlanta.
31. Emma Habersham, daughter of James Habersham II and Esther Wylly. She lived in Portland, Oregon.
32. Josephine dated it the 30th.
33. Josephine's brother.
34. Just north of Avon.

too, for my own amusement. Some funny dancing! A very amusing and nice time. Dr. Bonner came over for us. The three Newells and Tom came in a boat, and returned that night to Montgomery with a Mrs. Hunliter. Mamma staying in town with John Bolton. Lilla danced twice at the party, and was engaged a third time. Anna danced every time. Little Mary Belle and I enjoyed the new style dancing of the two high men, six feet, two inches.

"There will come a time when three words uttered with charity and meekness shall receive a far more blessed reward than three thousand written with disdainful sharpness."
—Bishop Joseph Hall, "Meditations"

SOLACE AT CHRIST CHURCH

Winter approaches. Josephine returns with her family to Savannah with the joys and sorrows of the summer recorded in her little hand-made diary. As she closes the journal the future looks uncertain and is filled with dread, but she finds spiritual strength in faith. And this dread is in the hearts of all mothers whose sons still live to fight again as the storm settles for a while at Chattanooga and gathers force to break over Georgia in all its fury the next year.

October 1, 1863. Thursday. Sewed; seeing about J. C.'s clothes and things to send him. Dear fellow, I wish he had some home comforts. A nice delightful letter from him, of [September] 26th. Wrote to Mary Owens on 30th. Played Mr. Higham's overtures after tea. Wrote to Joseph Clay on 30th.

October 2, 1863. Another long and beautiful letter from my dear kind child, speaking of the heroic patriotism and determination of *every man*, each actuated by some feeling of revenge for injuries done to his own State, perhaps *family!* Bragg's force 40,000, Rosencranz's 70,000. The child suffers from hunger with the rest, but does not complain. He repeats again and again that he would not be anywhere else, and rejoices to be there! God bless my child and preserve his health and life.

Mr. Higham left this morning. He has not been very bright—quite unwell. Anna and the little girls are all alive for a ride on horseback this afternoon, with Captain Brooks,

Lieutenant Houstoun,[1] etc. A sweet afternoon. Busy about Joseph Clay's box. Feel doubtful about the prawn. A biscuit not to be bought in town; all made for government. Dear baby quite crazy after *me!* and the puppies which he calls so prettily, "Pup, pup!" How happy they all are in our sweet country home! When so many are deprived of home and comforts. We ought to be *thankful.* Reading *Contes Morales de Murmontet*[2] [*sic*], and am amazed at the *indecency* of one of the stories! *Professedly moral!* These French do odd things!

October 3, 1863. Wrote to Mde. Guyol. Practised a good deal. Took a long time to peel prawn to put in peppers to send Joseph Clay, and then found they were *so hot* they could hardly be swallowed. So have determined to send prawn *salted only.* His father bought a quantity of Sailor biscuits for him, and I will add oranges, sugar, and nice things put up in cans. Practised a long time today, Mozart and Haydn. Went to walk with the little girls. The little girls went with their father to fish. Caught a great many; had a nice fish dinner.

My boy says he has received all of my letters and one from Freddie of 31st August—a month, and more, old. Willy came out last night and had a pleasant visit. Wrote me a pleasant note today. Trying to get business in town. The little girls much amused with their nice books.

October 4, 1863. Sunday. A beautiful Sunday, rather cooler. Took a long walk with Neyle, and got covered with "Hug me closes" and Creepers. The roses are coming out prettily. The sick Sergeant has gone home. No Church, as Charles is with his parents in Roswell, or rather, gone to the battle field to try to find out something related to his brother's[3] death. It was a sad, *untimely* death, but oh! how

1. Lt. Patrick Houstoun was in Brig.-Gen. William Miller's brigade, Kilcrease Light Artillery (Dist. of Florida). *Official Records, War,* Ser. I, Vol. XLVII, pt. 2, p. 1073. He took part in the defense of John's Island, S.C., on Nov. 15, 1863.
2. Jean Francois Marmontel, *Contes Moraux.* These tales appeared originally in the *Mercure de France* beginning in 1756. They first appeared in book form in Paris in 1765. They were quite popular and appeared in many editions.

SOLACE AT CHRIST CHURCH   93

glorious to die for one's Country. I can imagine no higher destiny for a noble minded man!

October 5, 1863. Monday. Anna went in to school today most willingly, and I think will study and try to improve. She says she *rejoices* in the delightful rides *in* and *out*. Weather delightful. The little girls and I took a long walk over to the Marsh through a pretty road on Mrs. Tucker's place. They talked of their Clarkesville[4] walks all the way, and when we came home Lilla wrote a nice letter to Robert White.[5] Practised and read Boswell's *Johnson*, a nice book to read at all times. A long nice letter from our boy—almost daily now. Bragg quiet. Rosencranz fortifying himself in his already almost impregnable position in Chattanooga. Lee and Meade quiet. Batteries *playing* at Charleston, and preparations to shell the poor city![6] The vile wretches[7]— their courage is in their fire-shells! Certainly their means of success. Joseph Clay writes often because he knows it is an anxious time.

October 6, 1863. Tuesday. Practised a long time. Wrote a long letter to Joseph Clay and Mde. Guyol, one to Mrs. Cohen, sending J. C.'s key and asking her to get some things from the *Atlanta* trunk[8] for him. Not so cool. Neyle and Robert brought home four elegant Bass weighing, I suppose, all of them, 35 pounds each. Robert made us laugh bringing up two on his back, bending under them, and they flapping their wide tails. Held and played with Baby all the afternoon. He put on stockings sent by Sister Mary Elliott,

3. Capt. Thomas Edward King, killed in the Battle of Chickamauga, at 34 years of age, leaving his wife, Maria Clemens, with three children. See Bulloch, *op. cit.*, 93.
4. Habersham County.
5. The son of Maria Elliott Habersham White, Neyle's half-sister.
6. Charleston had been suffering bombardment at intervals since Aug. 22.
7. Perhaps her anger was increased by the fact that the Federals brought 600 Confederate prisoners from Fort Delaware to Morris Island, keeping them under Confederate fire in retaliation for a similar action of the Confederates, who kept Federal prisoners in Charleston after its bombardment began. See Wallace, *op. cit.*, III, 186n.
8. The *Atlanta* had successfully run the blockade before being captured. The reference here is probably to blockade goods brought in before June 17th, the date the *Atlanta* was captured.

and directly began to show them to all and to say "totter!"—
and he will show his sore finger and make believe to cry. He
grows more and more like Father, laughs exactly like him.
Anna pleased with school affairs.

October 7, 1863. Wednesday. Dr. J. C. has come to spend
a few days, is not at all well. *Loves* Vernonburg dearly, plays
much with "his boy," Camber. A nice letter last night from
J. C. to Anna, and two from his servant John to his Mother.

We got the trunk off in good order on Monday. Prawn,
oranges, biscuits, and clothing. Could scarcely get biscuits,
and there is a dearth of nice things. Eggs are $1.50 a dozen.
Butter $5.00 and $6.00 a pound. Sweet potatoes $100.00 for
eight [bushels]. Were it not for the quantity of work for the
soldiers I don't see how the poor women would live. Very
few sick in Hospital—none very sick. Little girls gone to walk
on the Bluff. Mamma and I must go too. Wrote J. C. last
night. Among the high prices coarse gingham is $7.00 a yard.

October 8, 1863. Thursday. Belle Cohen[9] came out last
evening with Anna. Very glad to see her. She is always cheerful, agreeable, and talkative. Took a pleasant walk this morning with little girls. Anna gone in to school. On return found
Dr. Joseph Clay. So glad to see him. He loves to visit Vernonburg. He will spend a few days to fish with Neyle. Yesterday
Neyle and Robert brought home four *big* Bass weighing
from 33 to 35 pounds each, and plenty of other fish. He
distributed them among the Batteries and officers.

October 9, 1863. Friday.[10] How quickly the month is
passing. Sewing and hearing Belle talk. Took a nice walk this
lovely weather.

October 10, 1863. Saturday. More fine Bass. Belle gone in.
Anna went to Montgomery with the fishermen. I sewed the
children's Nassau flannels.[11] Glad to have them. Two long

9. Daughter of Solomon Cohen. She married (1) Frank C. O'Driscoll and (2) Dr. E. R. Corson. Her mother was also named Belle, but it is assumed here that Belle was Anna's playmate.
10. Josephine dated it Oct. 10.
11. Meaning flannels that had been brought in a successful run of the blockade from Nassau.

letters from our dear boy. Read a little, practised a little. Little girls anxious to go in to school.

October 11, 1863. Sunday. Quite cool. Charles preached; looks badly after his visit to his parents in their distress. He dearly loved his brother, Captain King. Guerard dined here yesterday. Came before the fishing party returned, and I had to entertain him an hour. Was glad to give him some music. Charles had Habbie and Willie at Church.

October 12, 1863. Monday. Not well. Read and sewed. Anna, Robert, and Lilla gone in to school. Little Mary Belle alone here. Lilla delighted at the idea of going in so as not to be *behind* the girls. Nice letter from J. C.

October 13, 1863. Tuesday. Two letters from my boy, says he knows I will be anxious when I hear they are shelling one another, but that the infantry are all out of the way behind Hills. Shelling from Lookout Mountain (of Chattanooga) did not do much damage, and is not resumed. Batteries firing on one another in Charleston forts, preparing for bombardment of Charleston—the wretches. Wrote a long letter to our boy, the 13th. Anna staid in with her beloved Katana, and Robert with Habbie. Lilla goes in alone this week, unless Mary Belle goes, which is hardly worth while. I really must practise this nice weather. Heavy rain tonight, and will perhaps become colder. Fears about besieging Mobile not now entertained.[12]

October, 14, 1863. Wednesday. Practised two hours, Mozart and Beethoven (Duos). Took a delightful walk with Mary Belle and Mamma. Dear baby is so intelligent, has been walking alone for more than a week. He pats-a-cake, says "buttie" for button, pretends to cry, and will make one understand what he wants. Runs all around after oranges. Anna in

---

12. Though Mobile was comparatively quiet at this time the Federals kept an eye on it and saw some shipbuilding going on. *Official Records, Navies,* Ser. I, Vol. XXV, p. 653. Farragut attacked Mobile Aug. 5, 1864, and gained control of the bay on the 23rd but, as in the case of Charleston, the city held out until the end of the war. See Evans, *op. cit.,* VII (Ala.), 43-46.

town still with her beloved Katana. Lilla spent Nelly's[13] birthday with her. Mary Belle wants to go in for Ida's[14] birthday.

October 15, 1863. Thursday. Trying to sew a little on the Nassau flannel petticoats, but the temptation to be out of doors is great in this Autumn weather. Picked some lovely roses. Our orange trees, more than a thousand, look *beautifully.* Putting out fresh leaves and shoots. Neyle has discovered several more Lemon trees, some bearing and some more *sweet* oranges.[15] The soldiers have not stolen every fruit.

October 16, 1863. Friday. All day out trimming and sheltering plants, etc. from frost and grass—*superintending* it, of course. Tom taking the Mistletoe out of the Oak trees. I could cry over the big Oak in the yard which the Mistletoe killed. Practised and sewed *those* flannels. Two letters from J. C. Things as they were. The dear boy writes me I must not be anxious as they are sheltered *behind* the *hills* from the shelling on *both sides.* Reported that Burnsides is reinforcing Rosencranz,[16] and that Lee is after Meade in Virginia.[17] Enemy in Charleston Harbor very busily fortifying themselves, interchanging shells all the time, without much damage on our side. Anna came this afternoon, so glad to get back to Baby. She is indeed growing to be a big, tall, girl—looks very hearty.

October 17, 1863. Saturday. Mamma gone in with Neyle

13. Eleanor Green Johnston.
14. Ida May, Willie May's sister.
15. Most of the trees bore sour oranges.
16. Rosecrans sent several dispatches between Oct. 1 and the 16th. Burnside had advised him on Oct. 1, that "All my available cavalry will be put in motion at once, to operate with yours on the north side," but then Rosecrans heard no more from him for several days. *Official Records, War,* Ser. I, Vol. XXX, pt. 4, pp. 25, 26, 114, 230, and 270. Lincoln had written Rosecrans on Oct. 4th as follows: "If we can hold Chattanooga and East Tennessee I think the rebellion must dwindle and die. I think you and Burnside can do this. . . ." *Ibid.,* 79.
17. Lee again took the offensive, Oct. 9, and crossed the Rapidan, making a "concealed and circuitous route" in an effort to flank Meade, but Meade retreated beyond the Rappahannock. Yet another attempt failed as Meade again retreated. Evans, *op. cit.,* III, 425-426.

to see Katana. Servants getting on nicely cleaning the townhouse—carpets all down (as many as we did not send away!)—painted, etc., scoured. Busy *out of doors*—can't stay in this weather. Have read little beyond the papers this week, and *that* takes much time. Played with Neyle after tea until 11 o'clock. Have been helping the children with Lessons every evening—grammar, French, and English, etc. Reading in *Idylls of the King*. What a wonderful *clearness*, transparency of language!

Quite an excitement in town, as Government is seizing horses for Artillery.[18] Lilla interested in her school, and Mary Belle anxious to be at *her* books again. Got a note from Willie—quite well. Mamma came out this evening; looks tired. Music after tea.

October 18, 1863. Sunday. Mamma went to Church, and all the rest, but had to leave—suddenly sick. I joined her, and thought she would *faint*. Got her in the carriage and Robert got some water from the spring in his *hat*, which revived her. Came home—felt better on the way. The ride yesterday upset her. Katana in Church—quite grown, tall and stout. She is a sweet child. I am thankful Anna and she can be such sweet friends. Baby rejoicing in a buggy ride with Papa, who says he is in the seventh heaven.

Some reports about Lee's Army[19] not certain. The papers

18. This was in accord with the "Impressment Act" of the Confederate Congress, Mar. 26, 1863. *Official Records, War*, Ser. IV, Vol. II, pp. 469-471. Even before the regulation provided in this law the government had followed a policy of impressment, to the great annoyance of the citizens who were beginning to suffer shortages of food and other things. President Davis wrote Governor Brown on Nov. 26, 1862, urging Georgia to let the Confederate Army have all supplies "in excess of the quantity indispensable for the support of the people at home." *Ibid.*, 211. So strong was the sentiment against illegal abuse of this law in Georgia that the legislature passed an ·act on Dec. 14, 1863, providing for punishment of from one to ten years of imprisonment for illegal impressment of property. *Acts of the General Assembly of the State of Georgia*, 1863-64, pp. 62-63.
19. Lee was in the Bristoe, Virginia, campaign at this time. See *Official Records, War*, Ser. I, Vol. XXIX, pt. 1, pp. 405-411. He was disturbed over the fact that a Richmond paper was publishing information about his movements. He declared the report was in error but warned that "information received by the enemy would serve to place him on his guard." *Ibid.*, 405-406.

quite exultant about Bragg's position. Heaven grant it may be all right! Oh what anxious times! Was up late last night writing to my child. My heart felt so drawn to him.

Reading Bishop Hall's works—delightful writer. Says of the Sabbath, "On this day I forget the world and in a sort, myself and deal with my wonted thoughts as great men use who, at some times of their privacy, forbid the access of all suitors. Prayer, meditation, hearing, reading, etc., etc., are the businesses of this day—which I dare not bestow on any work or pleasure but heavenly. I hate superstition on the one side and looseness on the other, but I find it hard to offend in too much devotion—*easy* in profaneness! The whole week is sanctified by this day, and according to my *care* of *this* is my *blessing* on the rest." How few of us keep the Sabbath as we *ought!*

October 19-20, 1863. Monday and Tuesday. Practised. Was a good deal out of doors. Mamma quite unwell. Anna, Lilla, and Robert gone in to school. Lilla is delighted with her *new* school-books. Sewed some.

October 21, 1863. Wednesday. All quiet at Charleston and Chattanooga Valley. Letters from our boy. Anna and Robert wrote him last night. Lilla quite unwell—upset by her drives to town. Riding *never* agrees with her. Mamma quite unwell.

October 22, 1863. Thursday. Much out of doors. Dear little Lilla very anxious for a *mullet* which her father is going to have got for her. Mamma's head is better. Baby so crazy to be *out* of doors that he can't take his usual naps. Is calling "Ma-a" and "pup-pup," all the time. Took him a nice drive in the buggy. Went with Neyle to see Major Hartridge at Rose Dew [*sic*]. His heart seems set upon the Orange trees there. Music after tea. Eddie Neufville[20] marries tonight, and Anna stays in to go to the Church. Bride not pretty.

October 23, 1863. Friday. Dear Lilla much better, Mamma also. Mrs. Gwantly, the sick soldier's wife, came to see me, and said she had no idea what her husband would have done

20. Edward Neufville married Mary Drayton Tattnall, daughter of Commodore Josiah Tattnall.

without my kind care. Well! it's something to do a little good. A long letter to Neyle from our boy—very interesting—about the President's visit to Bragg's Army. He says nothing of the squabbles of Bragg[21] and his Generals at all. Never talks of private affairs, but the *papers* make free enough. I wonder how it will terminate about Bishop Polk![22] Forrest considers himself overlooked, and is going to set up for himself. I fear Meade's Army has made good its escape[23] without being hurt at all by Lee, or very little. What a pity.

Picked beautiful roses. Quite an excitement about seizure of horses for Government. The children's hearts would break if dear Black Hawk had to be taken, and the aristocratic Black Eagle and dear little Caspar! I told Neyle Black Hawk would strain his sinews and nerves to the last behind an artillery wagon, and then die of a broken heart. Neyle arranged with a man that he would pay for any two horses he might buy—for Government use.

Things look brighter for our beloved Country. Mississippi is coming out finely. The enemy has a great drain with all the little armies it has to keep there! The loss of Vicksburg has produced nothing very beneficial for them. They can't attack Mobile, they are at somewhat of a standstill in Charleston, *preparing*, no doubt, for bombardment, but it is 103 days since they began the siege. Chickamauga kept them out of the heart of our Confederacy, and they are getting under shelter of Washington from Virginia. So things look bright, thank God. We were to make a visit to Montgomery to-day, but

21. Mrs. Chesnut took note of Bragg's quarrels and said she considered a general worthless who quarrelled with his subordinates. Mary Boykin Chesnut, *A Diary from Dixie*, edited by Ben Ames Williams (Boston, 1950), 316.
22. Though the fault was not entirely his, Maj.-Gen. Leonidas Polk failed to attack at daybreak as ordered by Bragg at Chickamauga, and Bragg had him court-martialed. But Davis soon reinstated him. He was killed in the battle of Kennesaw Mountain the next June. His greatest monument today is the University of the South, at Sewanee, Tenn., which he, with the help of Bishop Stephen Elliott and others, founded in 1860.
23. Meade not only saved his army but began his Mine Run campaign Nov. 26, thus disturbing the "winter quiet of Lee's camps." Evans, *op. cit.*, III, 427.

weather is dull—nice rain. Neyle has been catching plenty of bass, and distributing it with his usual generosity. Sending things to town gradually. House there quite clean and ready. Wrote a very long letter to my boys last night. Had a nice note from dear Willy.

October 24, 1863. Saturday. Rainy and cool. Lilla well, and disappointed in not having her "orangeade party" with the great favorite, Laura Kieffer,[24] and Mary Belle. The Communion Service which was stolen from the Keiffers' house has been restored, put back in the same place; but $300 taken from the poor man! What scamps these soldiers are to rob a poor man! One like themselves. Sat with Lilla, sewing. Anna busy fixing her things for town. Marion Morrel[25] and herself find it great fun to walk and meet Lieutenant Houstoun! Would not let Anna do this if I did not think it fit and right that a young girl should become accustomed to the society and attentions of gentlemen when young so that her head will not be turned by the first man who notices her!

October 25, 1863. Sunday. Rained. Did not go to Church. How *seldom* any of us stay at home! Robert rode on horseback to Church with Houstoun. Reading Bishop Hall. How true this remark: "There will come a time when three words uttered with charity and meekness shall receive a far more blessed reward than three thousand volumes written with disdainful sharpness." Another struck me, "Sin hath a guiltiness in itself that when it is seasonably checked it pulls in its head, and seeks rather a hiding place than a fort." *Again,* "The more familiar acquaintance we have with God the more we do partake of him. He that passes by the fire may have some gleams of heat, but he that *stands* by it hath the color changed. It is not possible a man should have any long conference with God and be in no whit affected. We are strangers from God. It is no wonder if our faces be earthly—but he that sets himself apart to God shall find a kind of majesty, an awful respect put on him in the minds of others."

24. The Kieffers were near neighbors at Avon.
25. She later married John Hammond.

Minded Baby a good deal, which gave him a *happy* Sunday!
October 26, 1863. Monday. A note from J. C., rain, rain, and hardship in Bivouac, but never complains. Anna and Robert talked of staying in town but now, as the time comes for going in, want to come back! Yesterday (Saturday)[26] Houstoun dined with us. Had nice crab soup and *old* time dinner! We *all* sang for him. He phillippined Anna.[27] Busy sending things to town gradually. In this way there is so little trouble, never any *fuss*—a thing I hate. The house being quite *ready* in town, it is easy to have all things fixed quietly.

October 27, 1863. Tuesday. The 25th of last year we moved to town. This year Anna and Robert go in *to stay* tonight. Anna sleeps with Katana, a grand thing for *her! Mary goes in to unpack the trunks and get the bureaus to rights.* Norah is very busy with the pantry and store-room stores. Baby and I play together, and he evidently thinks *something* is going on. A delightful letter from our boy, which I answered. The little girls busy packing their box of toys. One always kept for the purpose, and doll's clothes kept in. They brought it down stairs *themselves*—quite heavy. General Gist complimented Joseph Clay highly in his official report, saying "he had given most efficient aid to him during the heaviest fire, etc., etc."[28] I am thankful my child could do his duty so bravely. He has the right spirit and will display it whenever a chance offers.

October 28, 1863. Wednesday. Mamma went in this morning to *stay.* Rode in with Neyle—had got all her things nicely packed for town. The little girls and I meant to go to Montgomery, but, the weather being bleak and windy, I told them they had better stay, to which they agreed so pleasantly, al-

---

26. She meant "day before yesterday."
27. The word "phillippine" here refers to a custom, said to be of German origin, where, upon finding a double kernel in eating nuts, the lady and gentleman each eats one of the kernels, and one claims and the other gives a present or forfeit. See *Oxford Dictionary of the English Language.*
28. ". . . for valuable assistance in reforming commands, extending orders under heavy fires, and other efficient service." Brig.-Gen. S. R. Gist, commanding Walker's Division, Report, Chickamauga Campaign, Oct. 14, 1863, in *Official Records, War,* Ser. I, Vol. XXX, pt. 2, p. 247.

though much disappointed, that I sent for Laura to eat dinner with them. They played tableaux, etc., all day. When we got to the *pickets,* they turned me back because I had forgotten my passport, but John found it in the *clock,* and so we were at last off. The girls received me very pleasantly. Captain[29] and Aunt Hetty[30] had gone, to my disappointment, to Isle of Hope. So sorry. Coming back, the weather was delicious; a mild, balmy afternoon. John amused me by telling how one of his cousins had run off to the Yankees, but had had enough of it, and returned home gladly. The Newell girls were very pleasant indeed, so cheerful. It really is a delightful thing, this family good humor.

Well, it is my last *whole* day. How much I have to be grateful for! None of us sick—worth while. Mamma the only one indisposed, and she from a long drive! Dear Baby so hearty. Oh! I have very much to be thankful for. I went all round with John getting him to cover up plants, etc., etc., from frost, as Scipio is sick; and with Tom to show how I wanted the oranges and lemons picked. We shall miss the delightful shrimp, and fish, and crabs! Very busy all the evening fixing things.

October 29, 1863. Thursday. Neyle and two little girls said goodbye, leaving us, Baby, Dah, and Norah.[31] I busied myself and began a letter to Mde. LeVert,[32] which I must finish. Thank God for all his mercies to me and mine! I ought to have a grateful heart indeed. Goodbye pretty Summer home!

October 30, 1863. Home. Savannah. Got in in early time last evening. Baby staring at everything, particularly the down stairs and the carpets. It is very funny to see him. Up stairs he *peeps* from one room to another and *runs away*, scared. Thank God! We are all well. The little girls go to school today. Found everything comfortable and in order and place.

29. Captain Thomas Newell.
30. Hetty Adams, Captain Newell's second wife.
31. Norah Enwright Murphy. She and her sister Mary Enwright were Irish servant girls at "Avon."
32. Octavia Walton LaVert of Mobile, Ala., a cousin whose great-grandfather was George Walton.

How little trouble I have, how little confusion, because of the good servants. My husband is very generous to me in this matter. My dear room looks so sweet to me, and the dear little dressing-room so snug and cosy. Willy quite well, and very glad to see us come in. Mamma was quietly installed in her nice rooms.[33] I must try and *cultivate* a cheerful spirit. Went to see all at father's. Must not forget that Father came and spent last evening with us. We were *delighted* to have the beloved Grandfather.[34] He enjoyed his supper, and was so agreeable! How often do my eyes fill with tears when I recall my dear *Papa's* sweet image,[35] and longingly wish he could be with me and his dear grandchildren! How dreadfully he did mind little Sissy's death! It changed him much. It is very selfish to wish him back among us, when he has ended his life with its *full* portion of care and sorrow! Went to see them at father's, and was *going* to see Anna King, but she came *here*, with her children. I miss my dear Sister, Mary Ann![36]

October 31, 1863. Saturday. Went to the Shops, *frightened* at the prices of things—disgusted. Anna King takes it more quietly, being *used* to it—the *flaying*—$195.00 for a dress I could have got two years ago for just $9.00. One hundred and ninety-five dollars for a dress for Anna, for they would not cut ten yards for her. Sixty dollars for a straw bonnet for me—*untrimmed!* Dr. J. C. has been taking his meals with us. I was writing to Joseph Clay when Neyle came in, said he had seen the President,[37] and I had better go to the Masonic Hall to the "Shaking of hands." We did so—were much pleased with the affability of the President. He has a good, mild, pleasant face, not very remarkable, but thoughtful and, altogether, looks as a President of our struggling Country *should* look—care worn and thoughtful, and firm, and quiet.

33. Josephine's mother was in her 68th year.
34. Robert, Neyle's father.
35. Josephine's father died in 1855, at 65 years of age.
36. She was mourning the death of Mary Ann when she began her diary back on June 17th.

Anna and Willie had gone visiting, so had Robert. So they did not go.

Our piano was brought carefully in today, on *mattresses*—a nice way. Scipio has come in. Kate had a good cry because she had to go home sick. She is a good hearted creature, and I hope can come back. Norah and Mary like her, and they all get along well. Shells have been thrown into Charleston, *doing no damage*. The Sea face of Sumter is being bombarded. Rosencranz and Bragg in status quo. Lee quiet. Forgot to say that J. C. had run down to Atlanta. Wrote to get his winter trunk and prawn, etc. Wrote J. C. on 31st.

November 1, 1863. Sunday. Communion today at Christ Church. May I begin my winter with the help of God for my daily life, for I have a dull and wayward heart, and need his holy guidance in all things. Minded Baby, walked with him a little while on the Rail road track in Liberty Street, much to his delight, after Church.

37. Davis was at the coastal city inspecting the batteries. He arrived by special train from Atlanta, via Macon, at 8:00 Saturday, Oct. 31. Mayor Richard Arnold welcomed him with "an eloquent and appropriate address," after which he was escorted to his quarters at the Pulaski House. About ten o'clock, attended by Brigadier-General Hugh Mercer, Colonel E. C. Anderson, the Mayor, and other army, navy, and civil authorities, President Davis boarded the steamer *Beauregard* and proceeded down the river to view the fortifications. He went ashore at Thunderbolt and was received by the Phoenix Regiment, commanded by Colonel George A. Gordon. In the evening, following a torch light procession with band music and fanfare, a reception was held at the Masonic Hall. The President attended Christ Church on Sunday morning and left early the next morning for Charleston. See *Savannah Morning News*, Oct. 31, 1863, and Nov. 2, 1863, for account of Davis' visit.

> *"Ah, my poor princes! ah, my tender babes!*
> *My unblown flowers, new-appearing sweets!*
> *If yet your gentle souls fly in the air*
> *And be not fixed in doom perpetual,*
> *Hover about me with your airy wings*
> *And hear your mother's lamentation!"*
> —Shakespeare, *Richard the Third*

AH, MY POOR PRINCES!

THE high-water mark of Confederate glory had been reached at the end of summer in the year 1862 when Lee, with his lieutenants Jackson and Longstreet, drove Pope across Bull Run in the second devastating attack at Manassas Junction. But soon after came failure at Antietam. The end of the year brought victory for Lee again at Fredericksburg, and the spring of 1863 brought another victory at Chancellorsville—a costly one. Dead were one thousand six hundred and sixty-four Confederates, and Jackson! The tide had clearly turned in July at Vicksburg and Gettysburg. And yet the dying Confederacy rose to glory again in September at Chickamauga.

In October, reflecting on Tom King's death in the Battle of Chickamauga, Josephine had written in her diary "how glorious to die for one's Country. I can imagine no higher destiny. . . ." The real test of the sincerity of that statement confronts her the following year. Death would bring only despair to one of less courage, but her noble qualities overcome the baser instincts—humility replaces pride, contrition supplants hate, and faith triumphs over fear.

Josephine's diary ends abruptly when the William Neyle Habershams returned to Savannah to take up routine life in their town house. Their winter began with communion at Christ Church. Jefferson Davis was there, but Josephine made no reference to the fact that the President of the Confederacy had worshiped with her. She had attended a reception honoring him on the evening before and had recorded her anticipated pleasure in her diary, but her thoughts were centered on those closer to her as she worshiped in the family pew that first Sunday in November. Before another November came round this mother's anxiety for her boys had turned to grief.

As Josephine's diary closes, Rosecrans' Army of the Cumberland is bottled up in Chattanooga. Knowing full well that this strategic railroad city was the most vital point in the Confederacy, other than perhaps Richmond itself, Lincoln instructed Grant as commander in the west to break through at that point. Grant now had the advantage of able generals with which to drive the men in grey from Chattanooga. George H. Thomas took command of Rosecrans' Army and Sherman commanded the Army of the Tennessee. General Joseph Hooker, with the XI and XII corps of the Army of the Potomac, arrived in the theatre of operations and was placed under the operational control of General Thomas. On November 24, Grant ordered Sherman, Thomas, and Hooker to make simultaneous attacks. Sherman and Hooker pivoted on Thomas, Sherman on the left flank and Hooker on the right, in a double envelopment of Bragg's line. This maneuver was entirely successful. The capture of Missionary Ridge by Thomas' men was followed by Phil Sheridan's pursuit of the enemy down the eastern slope. The victory opened the way for a drive into Georgia the following spring. Joseph E. Johnston had replaced Bragg as commander of the Army of Tennessee and this had revived the spirits of the Confederate troops. This army was composed chiefly of two infantry corps commanded by Lieutenant-Generals William J. Hardee and John B. Hood and one cavalry corps under Major-General Joseph Wheeler. Walker's division and Gist's brigade were in Hardee's corps, and General Hugh W. Mercer's brigade had been assigned to Walker's division. Polk also brought his Army of Mississippi to join Johnston. Grant, who was made General-in-Chief in March, instructed Sherman to move against Johnston and penetrate as far as possible into the interior of the enemy's country and inflict all the damage he could upon their war resources.[1]

1. *Official Records, War*, Ser. I, Vol. XXXVIII, pt. 1, p. 3.

Sherman, then, with 100,000 troops set out from Chattanooga in May on his invasion of Georgia. His main armies were the Tennessee, now commanded by Major-General James B. McPherson, the Cumberland, commanded by Thomas, and the Ohio, commanded by Major-General John M. Schofield. Johnston, with only about 60,000 men, tried Fabian tactics in order to fret and harass the enemy, fighting only when a clear advantage was his. Such advantage appeared at Resaca and New Hope Church before the month ended, and Johnston fought defensive battles at those places. After the battle at New Hope Church, Willie expressed the general feeling of confidence in Johnston's ultimate success in his efforts to wear down Sherman's forces and make the North grow weary of war. Willie wrote to his mother on the last day of the month saying "there can be no doubt we shall be victorious." In the same letter he spoke of hearing a whippoor-will which reminded him of White Bluff but seemed strange to his ears, "for instead of hearing birds sing every morning, we hear shells and bullets whistling through the air, and all around us."[2]

After the battle of New Hope Church, Johnston's forces had worked their way south for eight miles toward Kennesaw Mountain. On June 4 they were ten miles north of Marietta. Willie was in Company F, 54th Georgia, Mercer's brigade, and there, bivouacked behind temporary breastworks, he wrote again to his mother. The march had been made through mud; rain had fallen intermittently for three days. Willie wished he could give Josephine information about the movements of Johnston's army, "but we are all in the dark."[3] A hint of the coming big battle at Kennesaw Mountain is seen in his closing statement: "There are 250 wagons loaded with hard tack and bacon, they left Atlanta a day or two ago, for our Army. I got this from a 'reliable' source—new wagons.

2. Josephine Habersham's Letter Book, p. 208. Hereafter cited Letter Book. This collection of letters and miscellaneous items is in the possession of Mrs. William Spencer Connerat of Savannah, Ga.
3. Letter Book, p. 228.

We cannot fall back much further, so these wagons may be for a long march in front."

Josephine received another letter dated June 5 in which her son said he was six miles from Marietta. He had seen Joseph Clay just two days earlier and found General Gist's mounted staff officer "extremely well."[4] The older brother, who had written so faithfully from Mississippi, now found himself too busy to write often, and Josephine had to be content with Willie's letters. Willie spoke of the condition of the roads, which had been made extremely muddy by the heavy rains—"the mud is actually up to our knees." It took the whole night to move the troops three miles. The men expected "the great Battle very soon."

The next day Mercer's brigade, having moved one mile during the night, was supporting Gist's brigade. This brought the Habersham brothers very close together. In fact, Willie wrote that day sitting in a staff tent of Gist's brigade.[5] It irritated the young private not to know what plans were being made to thwart Sherman. He was sure that if Johnston's "own coat knew his plans, he would throw it away."[6]

Robert, Josephine's third son, now seventeen, was in the Signal Corps stationed at Fort McAllister. Willie had heard that this corps would be disbanded and was afraid his young brother might join Johnston's army. He urged his mother not to let Robert come. "This life would not fascinate him much, and he had better seek service near home." As for himself, he said, "I have never regretted having come. I am perfectly content and satisfied with everything."[7]

Josephine received another letter from Willie, written before the battle and dated June 12. His company, along with five others, was sent out on picket duty a quarter of a mile in front of the breastworks. They protected themselves be-

4. *Ibid.*, p. 231.
5. *Ibid.*
6. *Ibid.*, p. 232. Davis, too, was growing more irritated at Johnston who was so afraid his plans would leak to Sherman that he withheld them from the President.
7. *Ibid.*

AH, MY POOR PRINCES   111

hind fence rails as best they could. Some "Yanks" were as close as six or eight yards. Firing was brisk. Willie and his companion fired several shots, "and if we did not kill them, made them change their quarters occasionally."[8]

From Chattanooga to Kennesaw Mountain Sherman had been making flanking movements aimed at cutting Johnston's communications, but decided to abandon these tactics and assault his enemy in a bold, but what proved to be a costly and unsuccessful, frontal attack. The Union commander described the situation in his report to Major-General Henry Wager Halleck, Chief of Staff. Three peaks forming a triangle covered the town of Marietta and the railroad back to the Chattahoochee. Kennesaw and Lost Mountain made the base and Pine Mountain the apex of the triangle. The summits of the three peaks were crowned with batteries, and the spurs were alive with men busy felling trees, digging pits, and preparing for the impending battle.[9] As the Union forces advanced the Confederate troops abandoned Pine Mountain and the line of breastworks leading to Lost Mountain, entrenching themselves at Kennesaw Mountain on June 17. A week later Sherman ordered the frontal assault, allowing three days for preparations. On June 27, McPherson moved forward at Little Kennesaw, and Thomas assaulted the mountain about a mile farther south. Both attacks failed. Johnston numbered his losses by the hundreds, Sherman by the thousands. Josephine's troubled heart was quieted when she learned her home was not among those saddened that day.

Sherman admitted his failure and assumed "the entire responsibility" for it. Though he recognized his costly error in judgment, he claimed that "it produced good fruits as it demonstrated to General Johnston that I would assault and that boldly."[10] He then resumed his flanking tactics, ordering McPherson to extend Schofield's line toward the Chattahoochee. General Schofield had gained a foothold across

8. *Ibid.*, p. 234.
9. *Sherman Report*, Atlanta, Sept. 15, 1864, *Official Records, War*, Ser. 1, Vol. XXXVIII, pt. 1, pp. 67-70.
10. *Ibid.*

Noyes Creek, southwest of Marietta. Johnston was forced to abandon Kennesaw Mountain, and before the month ended his losses were counted by the thousands. The toll for June was four thousand. Among the dead was the gallant Christian soldier and ranking Episcopal Bishop of Louisiana, General Leonidas Polk, killed at Pine Mountain. But Josephine was again spared any personal loss. Major-General William Wing Loring, who had been with Johnston at Jackson, Mississippi, now took command of Polk's corps as the beloved General was carried down to Atlanta for the big funeral at St. Luke's. The command later passed on to Lieutenant-General Alexander P. Stewart.

On July 9, Sherman, with three "good and safe points of passage over the Chattahoochee," turned his gaze southward where eight miles away over good roads lay Atlanta with its arsenals, stores, workshops, and foundries; where railroads converged from four directions. Advancement to the Chattahoochee had been his objective, but Atlanta "was too important a place in the hands of the enemy to be left undisturbed."[11]

After a short rest the whole army crossed the river on July 17 and moved toward Atlanta along the old Peachtree road. President Davis, who had never approved of Johnston's parry-and-thrust game of war, replaced him with John Bell Hood. General Hood did as was expected. He made two gallant attacks, one on the twentieth—the Battle of Peachtree Creek where he suffered the loss of 500 killed, the other on the twenty-second—the Battle of Atlanta.

The five hundred graycoats who fell on the twentieth brought sorrow to as many Southern homes, but the Habersham family was spared again. Josephine received a letter which Joseph Clay wrote on July 21. It was one of two letters written by her eldest son on that day, the day between the two big engagements. The letter began: "Willie and I are well." He then went on to say they had driven Howard's and Hooker's corps back to Peachtree Creek, but could not

11. *Ibid.*

drive them across. He sent "Love to all at home—to Pa and children and all—and Grandpa—to Robt, Anna, Lilla, Mary Belle, and Kisses to Little Camber from me." He closed by saying: "I am writing in haste, as Mercer's Brigade is passing— have just ridden ahead to see Willy—have just seen him. He sends love."[12]

The second letter which Joe Clay began that evening, and to which he added a postscript the next morning, again assured Josephine that "Willie and I are well." His brother was, even as he wrote, waiting to dine with him. They would talk of home as they shared the evening together. They would recall the fishing trips to 'Possum Point, picnics at Coffee Bluff, boating on Vernon River, the pleasant times at Avon. They would talk of the piano and flute duets played by their mother and father, the verses of the great poets read aloud. They would remember the "sociables" and the theatre in Savannah. But most of all they would talk of the family, old friends, the servants. "My love and Willie's to all at home," Joe Clay wrote, "to Grandpa, Grandma, Aunt Susan, Aunt Belle, all. Kiss the little children for us, and love to Pa and kind remembrance to Mary, Norah, Dinah, Fredericka, Tom, etc. Goodbye—my dear Mamma—many thanks for the Hymn —so appropriate and the beautiful extracts of poetry you have sent me—Goodbye." Then, reluctant to stop, he added, "It is now too dark to write longer—just received a very nice letter from you, dear Mama, written night of July 15th. Will give my letter to Willie—I have a good servant now—Goodnight —You will know when this reaches you if the Battle comes off tomorrow or not. I will not forget any prayers for safety of Willy and myself. Many, many thanks for your beautiful Prayer, just received. Love to all at home." Then next morning, being Friday, at daybreak he scrawled on the outside of the letter as he sat upon his prancing horse: "Willy and I are well."[13] The brothers separated about eleven o'clock that morning to form in line of battle.

12. Letter Book, p. 260.
13. Ibid., p. 225.

McPherson's Army of the Tennessee was the Federal force which received the brunt of the Confederate attack in the Battle of Atlanta, and it was Hardee's troops which launched the assault. Nevertheless, Walker's division was heavily engaged and suffered great loss. Willie, being in Mercer's brigade of Walker's division, and Joseph Clay, on Gist's staff, also of Walker's division, were two of the soldiers defending Atlanta and the homes beyond the city—even Avon down on the Vernon River where Josephine waited to learn whether or not "the Battle came off."

Though the battle resulted in terrible losses and though its final outcome, after six more weeks of siege, was the capture of Atlanta, it presents a fine example of "Johnny Reb's" sacrificial spirit, heroism, and fighting ability. The troops of McPherson's Army of the Tennessee attempted their usual flanking movement, but Hardee's Corps, with the aid of Wheeler's cavalry foiled the attempt and gained, before the day ended, a part of the Federal line. Hardee's trophies were eight guns and 13 colors, and Cheatham's division, which had played a major role in the battle, captured five guns and as many colors. General Hood said this engagement "greatly inspired the troops and revived their confidence."[14]

To Sherman and the Union the greatest single loss was the death of the courageous young McPherson, who, riding toward the southernmost division of General Blair's XVII Corps, came suddenly upon the Confederate line. When ordered to surrender he turned away, only to fall dead riddled by a volley of shots. Major-General John A. Logan took McPherson's command when he fell. Major-General O. O. Howard succeeded him later. To Hood and the South, especially Georgia, one of the great tragedies of the day was the death of Georgia's son, the gallant General Walker. Joe Clay and Willie's division commander set them the example of the hero's death on the eve of the fierce afternoon's battle when, caught by a shot from a picket's gun, he fell mortally wounded. General Mercer commanded Walker's division

14. *Official Records, War,* Ser. I, Vol. XXXVIII, pt. 3, p. 631.

during the battle, but later, brigades of this division which had lost heavily were assigned to other commanders. Thirteen of Walker's men had been killed together in a corner of a rail fence; Mercer's brigade had lost 168, killed and wounded; and Mercer, himself, had been wounded.

Josephine had wept many times in sympathy for those who mourned, but now she weeps because of the loss of her own. Joseph Clay was killed about three o'clock in the afternoon and Willie about an hour later. The mother was so grief-stricken at the news of Joseph Clay's death that the family feared to tell her of the double loss; but letters of condolence began to come and soon the full impact of the tragic day fell upon her. Lieutenant G. N. Johnston, of the Second Georgia Battalion "Sharpshooters," writing from Atlanta the next day said, "God only knows how you will bear this terrible affliction—this double affliction!"[15]

Lee Butler, Joe Clay's fellow staff officer and close friend who had gone through three years of hardship and danger with him, was able to tell Josephine how he died. Assuring the mother that her son was "universally loved by the whole brigade for his coolness and . . . gallantry upon the battlefield," Lee said, "He was killed at 3:00 p.m. in the front ranks, while encouraging the men to move forward. He lived but a few moments and suffered little, if any." His last words were typical of those who died in the arms of comrades: "Tell my Mother I die happy. I died at my post fighting for my country." After this he tried to say something more but could not be understood. "I had his remains carried off the field," Lee continued, "and would have accompanied them myself if it had been possible."[16] A news report from Atlanta, dated August 8, appeared in the *South Carolinian* telling how Lieutenant Habersham rode in front of the 46th Georgia assisting its gallant commander[17] in leading his men, waving his

15. Letter Book, p. 198.
16. *Ibid.*, p. 203.
17. This regiment was commanded by Major S. J. C. Dunlop. Its Colonel, P. H. Colquitt, had been killed at Chickamauga.

hat in one hand, his sword in the other. When within a short distance of the enemy, he leaped to the ground and rushed on, waving his hand and cheering.[18] Lieutenant Johnston said General Gist told him that Joseph Clay was "patting a soldier on the shoulder, telling him to stick to it" when the fatal shell exploded between them.

Willie, who had little taste for the glory of battle and less for the sting of death that sometimes goes with it, died no less courageously than his brother, who loved the risky business. Major Nathaniel O. Tilton, Quartermaster in Walker's division, wrote the boy's father on August 14 describing how his second son died: "William, seeing Captain Anderson somewhat in advance of his men, cried out 'Bully for our Captain!' and led with him; was one of the first up to the works. They drove the enemy out. This was the second line. The enemy fell back to the third line. . . . It was at this point that Willy fought so. He was cautioned not to expose himself, but determination glowed upon his fine countenance, and the only answer he returned was, 'When I shoot these last ten cartridges I will take care, not before!' "[19] Willie's good friend Lieutenant Charley Hunter was with him when he fell, and with the help of three others he buried the body late that night in a nearby field where it lay for three weeks.

Joe Clay's body was carried to Savannah and buried in Laurel Grove on July 27.[20] Robert went to Atlanta to try to secure Willie's remains but had to return home without success. Then on August 13 Major Tilton, with the help of Lieutenant Hunter, located his grave; and putting the body in a sealed coffin, he sent it to Savannah. There Willie's parents laid him beside his older brother with a single stone to mark their graves. On that white marble obelisk set on a square base is inscribed: *"In Their Death They Were Not Divided."*[21]

18. *South Carolinian.* Josephine copied this excerpt in her Letter Book (p. 209). The Columbia press was destroyed by Sherman's army.
19. Letter Book, p. 36. Capt. John W. Anderson, Jr.
20. *Savannah Morning News,* July 28, 1864.
21. Tombstone, Habersham Lot, Laurel Grove Cemetery, Savannah, Ga.

As would be expected, Josephine's heart reached out to Willie's friend who tenderly interred his body in its temporary grave. She wrote him a letter: "Your kindly offices for the helpless—the Dead—so touching to our mourning hearts and the tender sympathy you so feelingly express make a strong claim upon our affection! . . . I can but faintly appreciate the difficulties under which your noble work of love and charity was performed; but I know it was not postponed in the hour of weariness and fatigue and confusion incident to the close of a Battle!" All defiance and hate are driven from her heart by this traumatic experience. No longer does she speak of the Yankees as "those vile wretches." The enemy no longer wears a blue coat; the real enemy is War, and he wears a coat of fire. But there is no bitterness even against that enemy; there is no remorse, only humility and faith as she closes her letter by saying, "God is wise and just and good—infinitely good. . . . He knows what is best for us and for our children. . . . If this poor human heart suggests, in its misery, that *this is hard*, thank God for the restraining grace from on high which leaves the thought *unuttered, unexpressed*. Believe me, young friend, that the true secret of Life's happiness is to be able to say, 'Thy Will, not mine, be done'!"[22] The fire has burned out the dross and left only the fine and noble qualities of this aristocratic woman. Defeat has completed its disciplinary work. She remembered the family motto emblazoned on the Habersham coat of arms: *"In Deo Confide."*

Bishop Elliott wrote Josephine a letter of sympathy on July 26. Not knowing that she had been told of Willie's death he referred only to Joseph Clay, but Josephine had already learned of her double tragedy. The Bishop said, "I loved Joseph Clay so dearly for himself that I grieve for him as I have no other young person in the war. Joseph Clay was a noble fellow, brave as a lion, generous as a tender heart could be, affectionate almost as a girl, and so full of buoyant

22. Letter Book, p. 201.

life that it is hard to connect the idea of death with him. Most sincerely do I grieve with you, my dear cousin.[23]

Professor John LeConte, who had been Joe Clay's teacher and friend at South Carolina College, wrote for Mrs. LeConte and himself offering "heartfelt condolence" to the parents on this "two-fold bereavement."[24] He then went on to say, "You are aware that Joseph Clay left some of his books and other college relics in the custody of Josephine.[25] She has religiously taken care of them. When the poignancy of grief has been softened by time, a melancholy interest will attach to these relics of so devoted a son. At the proper time please instruct us what disposition to make of them."

Lilla, ten years of age, wrote a poem "For dear Mamma":[26]

> From our home we'll miss them sadly,
> When the winter's drawing near;
> Oh how sad it is to think
> That we will not have them here!
>
> From around our fire we'll miss them
> On a bleak cold winter's day;
> And we'll miss them in the country
> In the pleasant month of May.
>
> But they have gone to Heaven,
> A better place than here,
> With angels they are singing
> And they shed not a tear.

But the mother replied, using Tennyson's words:

> I sometimes hold it half a sin
> To put in words the grief I feel.

Yet, when in the privacy of her room, she cried in anguish:

23. *Ibid.*, pp. 201-202.
24. The letter was dated July 28. Letter Book, p. 212.
25. John LeConte had married Eleanor Josephine Graham ("Josie") in 1841.
26. Letter Book, p. 65.

> Ah, my poor princes! ah, my tender babes!
> My unblown flowers, new-appearing sweets!
> If yet your gentle souls fly in the air
> And be not fixed in doom perpetual,
> Hover about me with your airy wings
> And hear your mother's lamentation!

After stubbornly resisting Sherman for six more weeks, Hood surrendered Atlanta on September 2 and marched the Army of Tennessee back into the state from which it got its name, hoping Sherman would follow. He went first into Alabama, where he regrouped with militia from that state. Then, joined by Forrest's cavalry, he marched to Franklin where he encountered Schofield. Among the officers killed in this battle was General Gist, Joe Clay's staff commander. Normal military strategy would have made Sherman follow Hood, but he chose rather to march to the sea, bringing total war to the civilian population of Georgia. He had sent Thomas with his Army of the Cumberland to destroy Hood, which he did at Nashville in the middle of December. Sherman remained in Atlanta two and a half months. In order to make the city a military camp he ordered the citizens to leave their homes.[27] Thus began a confused and hurried evacuation of the strategic point that had been Sherman's goal. Before Christmas the Yankee general would reach another goal.

During this time we find Anna, Josephine's fifteen-year-old daughter, at Avon keeping a diary. The long entry for September 23 is devoted entirely to remembrances of her dead brothers. She wrote of Willie first: "Last Winter, the night before dear Willie went to the front, I went around with *him* telling all 'goodby,' we first went to Aunt Margaret Styles [sic], then Aunt Anna King's, then to Willie May's uncle's house, a pretty cottage, to find out if his company *was going* next day. There we saw at the front door, Willie May and Lieutenant Charley Hunter, who said Yes! they would have to go next day. We then went home, it was a *very*

---

27. Sherman to Hood, Sept. 7, 1864, *Official Records, War,* Ser. I, Vol. XXXVIII, pt. 5, p. 822.

dark night, I had poor Willie's arm, *we felt so sad*, for he was to leave next morning. . . . He did not go until that afternoon, I, Katana, Mamie Cohen, and the children, Papa, Uncle J. C. and Uncle John went down to the cars to see him off. Oh! to think that was the last time I saw him, he had been crying bitterly, and looked *so sad*. I kissed him, little did I think *for the last time*. . . ."[28]

Of Joseph Clay she wrote: "I remember *many many* delightful sails, I had with Joe Clay, about two years ago. I remember his coming from Tybee Island after being from home for months, jumping off his horse in the *happiest spirits*. He took us all, Ma, Grandma, Lilla, M. Belle, Dina, Norah, and Mary, Robert, all sailing by moonlight up the river. We sang, laughed, oh! dear J. C. was so very happy. And another evening he took me to Montgomery, and got the Newell girls, and Foremans, and took a most delightful sail by moon light. Miss Carter Bryan sang and played the guitar, oh what a most *splendid* evening we had, dear J. C. waiting on, and making every joke with the ladies, his bright face full of fun. Then another time, the Newells, myself, Bryans and Foremans, and *he* went fishing in a storm. As we got fixed, down came a pouring rain and thunder and lightning! We covered up under cloakes, etc, we were in the Steamer called 'Marie Louisa.' We went to Battersby's bath house, got in there from the rain and eat [*sic*] lunch, watermelons, etc!, we were *nearly* soaked. I believe dear Willie was with us. Then one afternoon *dear* Joe Clay rode horseback with me over to 'Coffee Bluff.' I was on Casper, *he* on 'Lot' (dear Willie's horse), we came home by a most exquisite moonlight, *riding very fast indeed*. I remember his saying I rode so well, and so kind in telling me how to manage. I think it was one of my pleasantest rides, I shall never forget it. . . ."[29]

Then, Sunday—"We have just returned from Church.

28. *Journal of Anna Wylly Habersham*, 1864 (Savannah, 1926), pp. 13-14. Permission to quote, granted by Mrs. George Noble Jones, is gratefully acknowledged.
29. *Ibid.*, pp. 14-15.

Uncle Charley preached a beautiful sermon, very affecting, *brought tears to my eyes*, it was about the religious feeling in our army for the last year, spoke of how *many* homes were *desolated* now, and how many young men had been called off, but were all *ready* to die. Said he knew of *two* young men, who died in defence of their country, and knew that they were ready for Heaven. I thought of my darling brothers...."[30]

In the middle of November Sherman burned Atlanta and set out with 60,000 troops on his destructive march to the sea, allowing his foragers to take $20,000,000 worth of property as they went, and permitting them to destroy other property which he valued at $80,000,000. Cutting a path 300 miles long and 60 miles wide, he personally supervised the destruction of 265 miles of railroad. He admitted that his troops were "a little loose in foraging," but contended that if "this may seem a hard species of warfare, . . . it brings the sad realities of war home to those who have been directly or indirectly instrumental in involving us in the attendant calamities."[31] By this time Hardee had been given the command of the department of South Carolina, Georgia, and Florida, and Cheatham had been given command of Hardee's corps.

On December 10, Sherman emerged at Savannah and three days later the Union flag was hoisted at Fort McAllister. Hardee refused an offer of surrender on the eighteenth, and on the twenty-first, as the Federal gunboats assisted in subduing the batteries at Rose Dhu, Beaulieu, Wimberly, Thunderbolt, and Bonaventure, the Union army marched into Savannah. Hardee, meanwhile, had managed to evacuate his troops across the river into South Carolina, much to Sherman's chagrin. But Sherman had reached his destination, and he presented to Lincoln "as a Christmas gift," the city, with its guns and cotton.

The *Water Witch* was burned by her crew at White Bluff to keep her from falling into the hands of the Yankees

30. *Ibid.*, p. 15. Entry of Sept. 26, 1864.
31. *Official Records, War*, Ser. I, Vol. XLIV, p. 13.

from whom it had been captured by Commander Pelot and his men in their daring raid. Its barnacled hull was a reminder to the family at Avon of the days of glory when spirits were high.

Sherman advised General Wheeler that "no provision has been made for the families in Savannah and many of them will suffer from want—and I will not undertake to feed them."[32] The Northern General's words were sometimes harsher than his deeds. For instance, when he started out on his march to the sea he had written Halleck: "We will remove and destroy every obstacle—if need be, take every life, every acre of land, every particle of property. . .";[33] but soon after telling Wheeler he would not feed the Savannah people he instructed his quartermaster to give "temporary relief" to the needy.

Northern friends began to send food and badly needed articles to the Savannah people. Aid was solicited in Northern cities by the super-salesman and crusader, Colonel Julian Allen of New York. He was assisted in Boston by Edward Everett. In Philadelphia the Episcopal Bishop Alonzo Potter made a successful appeal to the citizens for donations.[34] On January 18, a vessel named the *Rebecca Clyde* arrived from New York with supplies; two days later the *Daniel Webster* arrived with a cargo from Boston and New York, and on the following day the *Greyhound* came.[35] These ships brought flour, hams, salt, codfish, lard, vegetables, bread, fresh beef, and other articles. But by this time Sherman was making preparations to move into South Carolina, leaving the citizens of Savannah free to clear the channels of wreckage, and to restore, as best they could, their normal way of living.

Josephine was glad the river channels would be opened again to carry the necessities of life to her neighbors. And she was glad, too, that the young folks could once more sail the beautiful Vernon River in the moonlight. But she knew

32. *Ibid.*, p. 800.
33. *Ibid.*, Vol. XXX, pt. 3, p. 698.
34. See John P. Dyer, "Northern Relief for Savannah during Sherman's Occupation," *Journal of Southern History*, XIX, 465-468.
35. *Savannah Republican*, Jan. 19-22, 1865.

the receding tide was taking away something that could never return. She could not have known it, but perhaps she sensed the tragic fact that this war, which had destroyed so much, also destroyed her male progeny. Two sons had died in infancy, and "Jamesie" died at the age of seven. Now the war had taken Joe Clay and Willie. What of the two remaining sons, Robert and Edward? Could she have looked down the years she would have seen that Edward lived his life out unmarried; and that Robert, who later married twice, had only one child—a daughter. Thus, there went out with the tide the family name of Habersham. It was to live in America only in the name of a county in Georgia, in the name of streets in our cities, and a road as far away as Atlanta; and, perpetuated by patriotic societies, it would live in the memory of people who revere the past.

All the food that Sherman's "bummers" had taken would not satisfy Josephine's hunger. If, somehow, the Northern general had the power to restore all that his foragers had destroyed and should make Georgia prosperous and bountiful again he could not bring back what went out with the tide. Hers was not the physical hunger, she mused, as she stood upon the piazza at Avon and looked out upon the charred wreckage of the *Water Witch* protruding from the shallow channel of the Vernon River at ebb tide.

INDEX

Adams, Hetty 102
Agatha's Husband, 37, 40
Allen, Julian, 122
Anderson, Captain John W., Jr., 116, 116n
Anderson, Major Robert, 82
Antietam, Battle of, 107
Antony and Cleopatra, 23
Arabian Nights, 55
Army of the Cumberland, 109, 119
Army of Mississippi, 108
Army of the Ohio, 109
"Army of the Potomac," 15
Army of ·Tennessee, 14, 108, 119
Army of the Tennessee, 109, 114
Arnold, Dr. Richard Dennis, 85
Atlanta, 109, 119, 121
Atlanta (Fingal), 22, 26n, 29, 34, 40, 84, 93
Atlanta, Battle of, 83n, 112, 114
Aurora Floyd, 83
Avon Hall, 2

Banks, General Nathaniel P., 45
Barnwell, Mary Gibbes, 25n.
Barrington Hall, 9
Barrow, Elfrida De Renne, 3
Battersby's Bath House, 120
Battery Gregg, 79, 81
Beaulieu ("Bewlie"), 3, 121
Beauregard, General Pierre Gustave Toutant, 48, 52
Beethoven, Ludwig van, 1, 62, 79
Big Black River Bridge, 28
Big Ogeechee River, 3
"Black Eagle" (a horse), 99
"Black Hawk" (a horse), 72, 99
Blackwood's Edinburgh Magazine, 64

Blair, Major-General Francis Preston, 114
Blockade goods, 61, 94, 96
Bolton, Mary, 7
Bolton, Robert, 4
Bompiani, Roberto, 6
Bonaventure, Battery at, 121
Bonaventure Cemetery, 7
Bonner, Dr. M., Assistant Surgeon, C.S.A., Terrell Artillery, 47, 50, 55, 58, 78, 85, 88
"Bonnie Doon," 35n
Boswell, James, 93
Brackett, W. M., 59n.
Bragg, General Braxton, 44, 57, 67, 82, 83. 86, 91, 99, 104, 108
Brooks, Captain John W., 66, 91
Brown, Katy Roberts, 29
Bryan, Carter (Miss), 120
Bryan, Major Henry ("Harry"), 81
Bull, Ole, 11
Bull Run, Battle of, 107
Bulwer-Lytton, Edward George Earle Lytton Bulwer, 65
Burnside Island, 3
Burroughs, Benjamin, 2
Burroughs, Mrs. Joseph, 33
Burroughs, Laura, 5
Butler, Lee, 24, 115

Camber, Ann Sarah, 7
Campbell, Sarah, 17
Carmichael, William P., 25
"Caspar" (a horse), 99, 120
Chancellorsville, Battle of, 107
Charleston, S. C., 41, 43, 50, 70, 72, 86, 93, 95, 96
Chatham Artillery, 48, 66
Chattanooga, Tenn., 74, 82, 108, 111

124

INDEX 125

Cheatham, Brigadier-General Benjamin Franklin, 114
Cheatham's Division, 114
Chesnut, Mary Boykin, 99n
Cheves, Langdon, 41
Chickamauga, Battle of, 78, 80, 99, 107
Christ Church, 5, 104
Clark, Ruben G., 48n
Clarksville, 48, 93
Cobb, Brigadier-General Thomas R. R., 16
Coffee Bluff, 3, 40, 59, 120
Cohen, Belle, 94n
Cohen, Mamie, 44, 47
Cohen, Octavus, 35n
Cohen, Octavus, Jr., 35, 39
Coleman, Susan Ellen Habersham, 30, 41
Coleridge, Samuel Taylor, 29
Colquitt, Governor Alfred H., 17
Colquitt, Walter Wellborn, 17
Columbia College (see South Carolina College)
Comedy of Errors, 83
Conscription Act (Confederate), 59n
Constantine's House, 87-88
Contes Moraux, 92
Corson, Dr. E. R., 94n
Craik, Dinah Maria Mulock, 37n
Cranch, Christohper Pearse, 11
Cumming, Montgomery, 68

A Diary from Dixie, 99n
Dancing 87-88
Daniel Webster, 122
Davis, Jefferson, 103, 104n, 107, 112
Delegal family, 3
Dillon, Mrs. John R., 44n
Dinah (Negro servant), 40, 35n, 102
Dwight, John, 11

Edith's Ministry, 41
Edward's Depot, 42
Elliott, Charlotte, 46
Elliott, Jonnie, 61
Elliott, Leila, 60
Elliott, Mary Habersham, 59n
Elliott, Lieutenant Robert Habersham, 59, 65
Elliott, Saida, 61

Elliott, Bishop Stephen, 7, 68, 117
Elliott, Major Stephen, Jr., 69n
Episcopal Orphans' Home, 14
Everett, Edward, 122

Fogle, Theodore F., 36n
Forrest, Lieutenant-General Nathan Bedford, 119
Fort McAllister, 3, 110, 121
Fort Hudson, 34, 57
Fort Pulaski, 3, 4
Fort Sumter, 41, 67, 69, 72, 80-82, 82n
Fort Wagner, 50, 57, 58, 72, 79, 81
Fort Wimberly, 3, 121
Fredericksburg, Battle of, 107
Fulton, William, 63

Genesis Point, 3
George White's Academy, 18
Georgia Society of Cincinnati, 11
Georgia Society of the Colonial Dames of America, 22n
Gettysburg, Battle of, 36, 107
Gibbes, Leonard Y., 41n
Gibbons, William Heywood, 68n
Giles, Major John R., 38
Gilliam, Georgia, 60
Gillmore, Major-General Quincy A., 69n, 70
Gist, Brigadier-General States Rights, 15, 28n, 52, 80, 101, 108, 110, 114, 116
Gist, Captain William M., 80
Gnospelius, G. A., 43
"The Grandmother," 13, 26, 47
Grant, General Ulysses S., 28n, 55, 108
Grantland, Seaton, 60n
Great Expectations, 60, 72
Green Island, 3
Greyhound, 122
Guerard, Edgar, 30, 39, 95
Guyol, Mme. Mathilde, 51, 92, 93

Habersham, Ann Wylly Adams, 7, 8, 97
Habersham, Anna Wylly, 17, 40-41, 80, 84, 88, 93, 95, 119
Habersham, Edward Elliott Camber, 17, 53, 63, 66, 104

Habersham, Elizabeth Matilda ("Lilla"), 17, 80, 81, 84, 95, 98
Habersham, Emma, 87
Habersham, Esther, 7
Habersham, Frances, 9
Habersham, Frances Hazlehurst, 71
Habersham, James, 6, 7
Habersham, James Edward ("Jamesie"), 14, 66
Habersham, John Bolton, 9, 87
Habersham, John Rae, 65
Habersham, Dr. Joseph Clay (Josephine's father), 7, 53
Habersham, Dr. Joseph Clay (Josephine's brother), 8, 36, 44, 49, 58, 77, 94
Habersham, Joseph Clay (Josephine's son), 14-16, 22n, 23, 52, 58, 69, 71, 73, 80, 85, 91, 96, 101, 110, 112, 113, 114, 119
Habersham, Josephine Clay, 8-9, 12-13, 18, 107, 117-118, 122
Habersham, Josephine Elizabeth ("Sissy"), 14, 66, 84
Habersham, Joesphine Vernon, 87
Habersham, Mary Ann, 9, 21, 103
Habersham, Mary Isabella ("Mary Belle"), 17, 58, 81, 84
Habersham, Mary Butler, 8
Habersham, Robert, 2, 103
Habersham, Robert Beverley, 16-17, 95, 110, 116
Habersham, Susan Dorothy, 44
Habersham, William Neyle, 10-11, 52, 84, 85, 96, 98, 101
Habersham, William Neyle, Jr ("Willie"), 16, 23n, 79, 100, 103, 110, 113, 120
Habersham, William Waring, 9, 60
Hall, Joseph, Bishop of Norwich, 98, 100
Halleck, Major-General Henry Wager, 111, 122
Hammond, John, 100
Hampton, Wade, Jr., 23, 24.
Hannan, W. T., 16
Hardee, Lieutenant-General William J., 108 114, 121
Harden, William, 39n
Harden, William D., 39n
Harris, Francis, 10
Harrison, Colonel George Paul, 42

Harrison Regimental Hospital, 38, 48
Harrison's Regiment, 36
Hartridge, Colonel Alfred Lamar. 3, 31, 78
Hayden, Franz Joseph, 61, 92
Hazlehurst, Frances, 9, 71
Healy, George Peter Alexander, 6
Heir of Redclyffe, 30
Hemans, Felicia Dorothea, 21
Henry the Eighth, 51
Higginson, Thomas Wentworth, 11
Higham, Thomas, Jr., 23, 27, 31, 37, 50, 74, 83, 86, 91
Hill, Lieutenant-General Ambrose Powell, 85
Hilton Head, S. C., 34
Hood, Major-General John Bell, 108, 112, 119
Hooker, General Joseph, 34, 36
"The Hour of Death," 21
Houstoun, Patrick, 2
Houstoun, Lieutenant Patrick, 92, 101
Hover's Store, 67
Howard, Major-General Oliver Otis, 114
Huger, Joseph Alston, 59n
Hugo, Victor, 43, 45
Hunter, Lieutenant Charles C., 49, 116, 119

Idylls of the King, 97
Impressment Act (Confederate), 97n
Independent Presbyterian Church, 5
"In Memoriam," 54
Isle of Hope, 44, 51, 69, 102

Jackson, Miss, 43, 47, 57
Jackson, Lieutenant-General Thomas Jonathan 52, 64, 107
James Island, 15, 30
Jews, persecution of, 64
John (Negro servant), 71
Johnston, General Albert Sidney, 42n
Johnston, Eleanor Green, 96n
Johnston Lieutenant George N., 72, 115, 116

Johnston, General Joseph Eggleston, 23, 55, 108, 109, 111
Jones, George Fenwick, 6, 17
Jones, George Noble, 8, 17
Jones, Sarah Campbell, 6
Jones Fort, 3

Kennesaw Mountain, Battle of, 109, 111, 112
Kieffer family, 2
Kieffer, Laura, 100
Kieffer, George H., 63
King, Anna Habersham, 35
King, Charles Barrington, 8, 43, 78, 79, 87, 92, 121
King, Katana, 87n, 95, 97, 101
King, Mallery Page, 24
King, Captain Thomas, 9, 92, 93n, 95, 107
King Lear, 51, 60
Kollock, Dr. Phineas Miller, 43n
Kuhlau, Frederick, 39n

LaCoste, Henri, 29, 29n
LaCoste, Marie, 29n
La Roache, Nelly, 62n
Laurel Grove Cemetery, 7
LeConte, Eleanor Josephine Graham ("Josie"), 118
LeConte, John, 14, 118
LeConte, Julian ("Jerry"), 39n, 41
LeConte, William, 39n
Lee, Robert E., 3, 24, 34n, 36, 44, 53, 57, 64, 67, 73, 96, 97, 104, 107
Lessing, Felix, 11, 61, 62n
Le Vert, Octavia Walton, 102, 102n
Life of Lord Chancellor Eldon, 54n
Life of Samuel Johnson, 93
Lincoln, Abraham, 107, 121
Little Ogeechee River, 3
Logan, Major-General John A., 114
Longfellow, Henry W., 11
Longstreet, Major-General James, 82, 85, 107
Lookout Mountain, Battle of, 95
Loring, Major-General William Wing, 112
Lost Mountain, 111
"Lot" (a horse), 120
Lovell, Major-General Mansfield, 51n
Low, Andrew, 22n

Low, Mary Stiles, 22, 25

McAllister, Emma, 48
McAlpin family, 3
Macbeth, 49, 51
McKeever, Harriet B., 41n
McPherson, Major-General James B., 109, 111, 114
Madame Chegare's French School,, 18
Manassas Junction, 107
Manigault, Frances Habersham, 27
Manigault, Louis, 10, 66, 70, 73, 74, Marietta, Ga., 109, 110
Marmontel, Jean Francois, 92
Maximilian, Archduke, 70n
Maxwell, Mary Elizabeth Braddon, 83
May, Ida, 40n, 96
May, William H., 40, 81
"May Queen," 23
Meade, General George G., 36, 96
Mercer, Brigadier-General, Hugh W., 78, 108.
Mercer's Brigade, 109, 110, 113, 114
Millekin's Bend, Miss., 28
Mexico, 70
Les Miserables, 43n, 65
Missionary Ridge, Battle of, 108
Mobile, Ala., 95, 99
Montgomery, General Richard, 2
Montgomery Cross Roads, 2, 5, 58, 79, 94, 99
More, Sir Thomas, 54
Morgan, Brigadier-General John H., 55, 57
Morrell, Marion, 72, 100
Morris Island, 45, 50, 53, 67, 73, 74, 79, 80, 83
Mozart, Wolfgang Amadeus, 61, 62, 79, 92
Murphy, Norah Enwright (Irish servant girl), 102

Napoleon III, 70n
Nashville, 16
Nassau, 61, 94
Nephew, Catherine Margaret, 9
Neufville, Edward Frank, 44, 98
New Hope Church, Battle of, 109
New Orleans, La. 42
Newell, Mary Wylly, 49, 87

Newell, Captain Thomas, 102
Neyle, Elizabeth, 8
Northern aid, 122
Noyes Creek, 112
Nungezer family, 2
Nuttall, Mary Savage, 17

O'Brien, Mary, 8
Ocean Steamship Company, 17
O'Driscoll, Frank C., 94n
Oglethorpe, James Edward, 1
Olmstead, Colonel Charles H., 3, 4
Owens, George Watkin, 65
Owens, Mary, 51, 64, 65, 91

Peale, Rembrandt, 6
Pelot, Lieutenant-C o m m a n d e r Thomas P., 37n, 122
Pemberton, Lieutenant-G e n e r a l John Clifford, 28n, 52
Pericles, 79
Phelps, Y. U., 14
Le Philosophe Sous les Toits, 58
Pine Mountain, 111
Pocataligo, S. C., 41
Polk, Major-General Leonidas, 99, 112
Pope, Major-General John, 107
Port Hudson, 45
'Possum Island, 3
Potter, Bishop Alonzo, 122
Prices, 74, 94
"Pulaski Guards," 15
Pulaski House, 62

Rae, Isabella, 8
Rattlesnake (see *Nashville*)
Read, Captain John, 15
Rebecca Clyde, 122
Resaca, Battle of, 109
Rhett, Colonel Alfred, 69
Richmond, Va., 34, 108
Ringgold, Ga., 84
Ripley, Brigadier-General Roswell Sabine, 48, 52
Rogers, Caroline, 72
Rome, Ga., 80, 81, 82, 84
Romeo and Juliet, 60
Roper, William, 54n
Rosecrans, General William Starke, 57, 74, 82, 83, 85, 86, 91, 96, 104, 108
Rose Dhu, 2, 67, 121
Roswell, Ga., 80, 87

Round Hill School, 11
Rubens, Peter Paul, 73

"*St. Agnes' Eve*," 25
Saint John's School, 14
Saint Luke's Episcopal Church, 112
Sand Hills (Augusta), 30
Savage, Thomas, 6
Savannah, 1, 102, 121
"Savannah Cadets," 16
"Savannah Guards," 14
Scharf, John Thomas, 17
Schiller von Johann Christoph Friedrich, 29
Schlegel, August Wilhelm, 83n
Schlegel, Friedrich, 83n
Schley, Georgia Maria, 17
Schley, John, 3
Schley, Margaret Cunningham, 16
Schley, Sallie, 87
Schofield, Major-General John M., 109, 111
"Scipio" (Negro servant), 71, 101, 102, 104
Scott, John, First Earl of Eldon, Lord Chancellor, 54
Screven, Colonel John, 12
Screven, Mary, 34, 38
Shakespeare, William, 1, 23, 51, 60, 83
Sherman, Major-General William Tecumseh, 108, 109, 112, 119, 121, 122
Sheridan, Major-General P h i l i p Henry, 108
Shortages, 87, 99
Simkins, Lieutenant-Colonel J. C., 53
Simkins, William D., 17, 53
Smith, Brigadier-General W. Duncan, 15
Snowden, William Etsel, III, 52n
"Somebody's Darling," 29n
South Carolina College, 14, 27
South Carolinian, 115
Souvestre, Emil, 58
"The Star and the Flower," 12
Stephens, William, 3, 7
Stewart, Lieutenant-General Alexander P., 112
Stiles, Florence, 70
Stiles, Sam V., 72, 87
Sumter (see Fort Sumter)
"Sunset on the Vernon River," 9

INDEX

"Tallulah," 14
Taming of the Shrew, 51
Tattnall, Josiah, 98n
Tattnall, Mary Drayton, 98n
Taylor, Lieutenant-General Richard, 42
Tennyson, Alfred, 13, 25, 26, 47, 118
Terrell Artillery, 53, 66, 72
Theatre, 40, 55
Theus, Jeremiah, 6
Thomas, Major-General George Henry, 108, 109, 111, 119
Thunderbolt, battery at, 3, 121
Tieck, Ludwig, 83n
Tilton, Major Nathaniel O., 116
Tom (Negro servant), 71, 84, 96
Torquemada, Thomas, 64
Twelfth Night, 37
Twiggs, Captain H. D. W., 51
Twiss, Horace, 54
Two Gentlemen of Verona, 83

University of the South, 17

Vernon, Admiral Edward, 1
Vernon, James, 1
Vernon River, 1
Vernonburg, 2, 94
Vicksburg, 22, 24, 27-28, 31, 38, 40, 42, 51, 57, 107
Villalonga, John L., 61n

Wade, Freddie, 22
Wade, Johanna, 9
Walker, Major-General William Henry Talbot, 28, 29n, 83n, 108, 114
Walker's Division, 45, 73
War of Jenkins' Ear, 3
Warfield, Louis, 78
Washburn, Eddie, 24, 28
Washburn, Ingersoll, 24
Washburn, Joseph, 9
Washington, D. C., 42
Washington, George, 8
Water Witch, 17, 37n, 121, 123
Wayne, Phenie, 78
Westminster Review, 65
Wheeler, Lieutenant-General Joseph, 108, 122
White, Robert, 93
White Bluff, 2, 109, 121
White Bluff Presbyterian Church, 2, 5, 63
Whitefield, George, 7
Wilkins, Gillie, 71
Woodbridge, Wylly, 70n
Wormsloe, 3
Wright, Sir James, 8

Yamacraw Bluff, 3
Yonge, Charlotte Mary, 30

www.ingramcontent.com/pod-product-compliance
Lightning Source LLC
Chambersburg PA
CBHW020805160426
43192CB00006B/449